How to Design a World-Class Engineering College

A History of Engineering at Carnegie Mellon University

How to Design a World-Class Engineering College

A History of Engineering at Carnegie Mellon University

by Leah Pileggi

Carnegie Mellon University Press
Pittsburgh 2013

About the cover image:

Paul L. Smith (B.S. Physics 1955, M.S. EE 1957 and Ph.D. EE 1961, all from *Carnegie Tech) teaches a class on Flagstaff Hill in the spring of 1961. Smith was assistant professor at Tech from 1960-1963. He went on to teach at the South Dakota School of Mines and Technology, where he is now Professor Emeritus of Atmospheric Sciences.*

Hamerschlag Hall is seen in the background. The white building is Jones Hall. It *was razed shortly after this photograph was taken, and the construction of Scaife Hall was completed by 1962.*

General Photo Collection, Carnegie Mellon University Archives, Pittsburgh, *Pennsylvania.*

Design by: Connie Amoroso

Library of Congress Control Number 2013930797
ISBN 978-0-88748-575-6
Printed and bound in the United States of America

10 9 8 7 6 5 4 3 2 1

to Larry & Hannah

—L. P.

Preface

In September of 2010, Dean Pradeep Khosla asked if I would interview some of the retired professors from Carnegie Mellon's engineering school, the Carnegie Institute of Technology (CIT). I spoke first with Steve Fenves and since then with many elder statesmen of CIT. Those interviews prompted me to research the entire history of engineering at Carnegie Mellon University (CMU) to find out how a humble technical school became one of the world's premier engineering colleges.

This story follows one narrow thread from 1900 to 2013. Because it is not a comprehensive history, many of the hardworking and dedicated faculty, administration, staff and students who helped to build and support CIT throughout the years are not specifically named. Perhaps someone else will take on that challenge.

I owe many thanks to many people. Thank you to Dustin Williams, Katie Behrman and Gabrielle Michalek of the Carnegie Mellon University Archives; Sherry Stokes, Chriss Swaney, Matt Coley, Sue Haslett, Bridget Decker, Kelly McQuaid, and Romayne Botti from CIT; Larry Sumney, president and CEO of the Semiconductor Research Corporation (SRC); the Institute for Jewish Research (YIVO) Archives; Beth Toor; Chris Hunter, director of Archives and Collections, Museum of Innovation and Science (miSci); Jim Duggan and Mike Whelan from the Edison Tech Center; Robert Fantazier from the Software Engineering Institute (SEI); Liz Lee; and Donna Beck and Matt Marsteller, CMU librarians.

Also, my thanks to present and former CIT faculty Kumar Bhagavtula, Jacobo Bielak, Dave Dzombak, Gary Fedder, Ignacio Grossmann, Chris Hendrickson, Granger Morgan, José Moura, Ed Rubins, Rob Rutenbar, Dan Siewiorek, Sarosh Talukdar and Don Thomas.

Special thanks to Dean Jim Garrett; former CIT Deans John Anderson, Steve Director, Angel Jordan, Pradeep Khosla and Jim Williams; and to retired CIT faculty Steve Fenves, Bob Mathias, Fran McMichael, Allan Meltzer, Harold Paxton, Wil Rouleau (a freshman at Carnegie Tech in 1947 and a presence on campus ever since), Joel Tarr and Art Westerberg.

To my husband Larry, I couldn't have done this without your support.

Contents

Presidents

Arthur A. Hamerschlag, President, 1903-1922
Thomas S. Baker, President, 1922-1935
Robert E. Doherty, President, 1936-1950
John Christian Warner, President, 1950-1965
H. Guyford Stever, President, 1965-1972
Richard M. Cyert, President, 1972-1990
Robert Mehrabian, President, 1990-1997
Jared L. Cohon, President, 1998-2013
Subra Suresh, President, 2013-

Deans of Engineering

Arthur A. Hamerschlag, Dean of Engineering, 1903-1908
John Hopkin Leete, Dean of Engineering, 1909-1917
William Elton Mott, Dean of Engineering and Science, 1917-1932
Webster Newton Jones, Dean of Engineering and Science, 1933-1953
Benjamin Richard Teare, Jr., Dean of Engineering and Science, 1953-1965
William Wilson Mullins, Dean of Engineering and Science, 1966-1970
Herbert L. Toor, Dean of Engineering, 1970-1979
Angel G. Jordan, Dean of Engineering, 1979-1983
James C. Williams, Dean of Engineering, 1983-1988
Paul Christiano, Dean of Engineering, 1989-1991
Stephen W. Director, Dean of Engineering, 1991-1996
John L. Anderson, Dean of Engineering, 1996-2004
Pradeep K. Khosla, Dean of Engineering, 2004-2012
James H. Garrett, Jr., Dean of Engineering, 2013-

The Birth of Pittsburgh's
Carnegie Technical Schools

The history of the engineering college at Carnegie Mellon University—the Carnegie Institute of Technology—might be entitled *The Little Engineering College That Could*. What began in 1900 as a wide-ranging assortment of two- and three-year technical programs is now a world-class top 10 engineering college with an international presence.

Today, CIT research has a global impact over a wide range of topics, and it has campus affiliations as widespread as Portugal, Rwanda, Japan and China.

The prominence enjoyed by CIT today can be attributed to key decisions made by a small number of faculty and administrators, strategic funding, highly motivated and self-driven students, and an unusually adaptable teaching and research environment. But mostly, it was the people. Brilliant and devoted people. The right people at the right time, some of whom drove themselves on the university's behalf until they collapsed. They established the institutional DNA that drives engineering at CMU today.

Retaining its roots in applied engineering, today's engineering college bears the name of the university's earliest incarnation as a four-year degree-granting institution: the Carnegie Institute of Technology. And as the name suggests, it all started with a man named Carnegie.

Andrew Carnegie

By 1899, Andrew Carnegie was one of the wealthiest men in the world, living mostly in New York and Scotland. He had designed his own wildly successful life through hard work, an astute business sense and an eye for opportunity. Other U.S. iron makers saw "pig iron scale" as a liability; he retained a chemist to learn how to turn that "waste" into enormous profit. He had amassed much of his fortune from his iron and steel businesses in Pittsburgh, and now he spent most of his time giving his fortune away.

How did he decide which causes to support? The seeds of those decisions were planted early.

Carnegie's love for books and the world they opened up to him began at age 15. With no books of his own and no money to buy any, he was

delighted to learn that Colonel James Anderson (ironically, an iron maker and philanthropist of Scotch-Irish descent) was opening his personal library of 400 volumes to boys in Pittsburgh. These were boys whose circumstances did not allow them to be exposed to books, who worked to support their families instead of going to school. Carnegie was exactly one of those boys, with only five years of formal education (ages 8-13) at the Rolland Street School in his hometown of Dunfermline, Scotland. By the age of 15, having moved with his family to Pittsburgh, Carnegie was working long days as a telegraph messenger in order to help support his family. By the time of his death in 1919 at the age of 83, his early love of books had prompted him to build more than 2,800 libraries worldwide.

Andrew Carnegie at 16 with his brother Thomas. Courtesy of the Carnegie Library of Pittsburgh.

As to the many millions of dollars he donated to educational institutions, his only personal experience with "advanced" education came in 1850 when he and a few friends met in the evenings with a bookkeeper to learn double entry bookkeeping. But he dreamed of attending a real university.

At the age of 33 in 1868, Carnegie wrote a memorandum on stationery from the St. Nicholas Hotel in New York. That memorandum was essentially a "bucket list." Among the items on his list was to retire in two years and never again to make an effort to increase his fortune, instead living off his annual salary of $50,000. He would then spend "the surplus each year for benevolent purposes." He followed through on the benevolent part. As to increasing his fortune? He just couldn't stay away from business, so his fortune continued to increase, dramatically. As to furthering his education, he wrote of settling in Oxford to "get a thorough education, making the acquaintance of literary men." He anticipated it taking "three years' active work."

C.C.No.931.

Pittsburgh, Nov.26th, 1900.

To the Presidents and Members of Select and Common Councils,

Gentlemen:-

I herewith transmit to your honorable bodies a communication received from the hands of Mr.Andrew Carnegie, under date of November 15th, 1900. In this letter Mr.Carnegie proposes that if the city of Pittsburgh will furnish a suitable site, he will provide all the money for a polytechnical institute. He will also endow it with $1,000,000 five per cent. gold bonds yielding a revenue of $50,000 a year. The management of the school and its endowment, Mr.Carnegie desires, should be undertaken by the Board of Trustees now having charge of the Carnegie Institute comprising the library, art gallery, museum and music hall. The proposition of Mr.Carnegie is hereby submitted for such action as Councils may deem proper.

In this connection I desire to say that the offer of Mr.Carnegie is one the value of which is beyond measure. We have continually before us the evidence of the great good that has been and is being accomplished by the generous gift he has already made to this city, the Carnegie Institute. The means of enjoying art, music, science and literature, with their educating influences, have been brought within reach of every citizen of Pittsburgh. They have been a great benefit to the present generation and it is beyond question that they will exert a powerful and beneficent influence over the generations to come.

A polytechnical institute, such as Mr.Carnegie proposes to establish in Pittsburgh, will be of unbounded benefit. To a manufacturing centre such as this its worth cannot be estimated. The Central Board of Education has recognized the need of such an institute and the magnificent proposition of Mr.Carnegie places within reach of the city at a bound what it would take a long time to obtain by the ordinary method of providing for the cost in the tax rate. Mr.Carnegie's only condition is that the city provide a suitable site with ample room for future extension to meet the certain growth of Pittsburgh. I trust Councils will accept this splendid gift.

Respectfully yours,

W.J.DIEHL, Mayor.

That formal education never happened for him, but when in 1900 the Central Board of Education of Pittsburgh asked the city of Pittsburgh for $100,000 to create a technical school, Andrew Carnegie was ready to step in. Here was a chance for him to combine his benevolence and his academic longing in his beloved city of Pittsburgh. He had donated millions to existing universities, but this would be a chance to start a brand new institution of higher learning literally from the ground up.

An academic at heart but a businessman to his core, he knew that as the 20th century loomed, the industries he had helped to create were changing. New manufacturing techniques were becoming necessary at a faster rate, and more employees familiar with technology were needed for expanding industries. Carnegie was keenly aware of other technical schools that had been founded at the end of the 19th century to educate a new generation of technicians and engineers, schools like Drexel Institute of Art, Science and Industry (now Drexel University); Pratt Institute; the Armour Institute (now Illinois Institute of Technology) and Worcester Polytechnic Institute. It was time for Pittsburgh—the center of his industrial world—to have its own.

Based on visits to other technical schools in the U.S. and Great Britain, Carnegie believed that many Pittsburgh students would attend classes at night after a full day of work. Carnegie professed his admiration for manual laborers and his belief that this new technical school "would develop latent talent around us to such an extent as to surprise the most sanguine." If only he knew.

In November of 1900, he promised to donate $1 million to found a technical school in Pittsburgh. It took almost five years before the first students walked into the classrooms of Pittsburgh's Carnegie Technical Schools. In the meantime, someone would have to do a lot of work. Because Carnegie no longer lived in Pittsburgh, it would have to be someone pretty amazing.

The Key to Success—Choosing the Right People

Andrew Carnegie admitted that he wasn't an expert in many fields. His success, he believed, was due in large part to his ability to run an organization by choosing the right people. It started with rabbits.

As a boy, he raised rabbits at his home. Having no money, he convinced other boys to help gather food for the baby bunnies by telling them that he would name a rabbit after each of them. He realized in later life that he probably took advantage of those boys, but it was clear that even at an early age, he had a knack for organization:

I treasure the remembrance of this plan as the earliest evidence of organizing power upon the development of which my material success in life has hung—a success not to be attributed to what I have known or done myself, but to the faculty of knowing and choosing others who did know better than myself. Precious knowledge this for any man to possess. I did not understand steam machinery, but I tried to understand that much more complicated piece of mechanism—man. (Carnegie, 25)

Who would he choose to guide his new technical school?

Carnegie Institute, 1908, with the first of Carnegie Tech's buildings rising behind it (near smokestack). Courtesy of the Carnegie Library of Pittsburgh.

Finding the Right Engineer for the Job

The Board of Trustees of the Carnegie Institute—Carnegie's gift to Pittsburgh of a library, museum, music hall and fine arts complex—had been chosen by Carnegie himself. The members of that board were now charged with finding the right people to help guide the new technical school. During 1901, they brought a committee of educational consultants to Pittsburgh to discuss the direction and focus of the new school. The consultants came from Cornell University, Armour, Rose Polytechnic Institute

17

and the University of Wisconsin. They proposed a plan, but it was rejected as being too ambitious in terms of land required, and it was not connected enough to what was needed at that time in Pittsburgh for technical education.

In 1902, another group of consultants was brought in. But before they could issue a proposal, a 32-acre site adjacent to the Carnegie Institute was chosen as the location of the new school. In February 1903, taking into consideration the location and limited space now determined for the campus, the second group of consultants set forth its more realistic recommendations, and those were received and approved by the board. That group of consultants included men from Pratt Institute and the Allegheny Manual Training School, and also included a 31-year-old technical education specialist from St. George's Trade School in New York City named Arthur A. Hamerschlag. An engineer by trade who never attended college, he would become the first director and the guiding force behind the formation of Andrew Carnegie's creation.

Arthur A. Hamerschlag

Arthur Arton Hamerschlag was born in New York City in 1872. His father was a chemist who had immigrated to the United States from what was then Bohemia (later Czechoslovakia, now the Czech Republic). His parents were Austrian Jews who converted to become Episcopalians, attending St. George's Episcopal Church in New York.

As a child Hamerschlag attended public schools, but in 1886 at the age of 14, he began to attend the newly formed Hebrew Technical Institute. It had been founded to encourage poor Jewish youth to consider careers in the practical arts. The boys studied subjects such as mechanical drawing, woodworking, metalworking, instrument making, auto mechanics and electricity. They went on to work as mechanics, sign painters, electricians, plumbers and carpenters. During his time there, or shortly after he graduated from the three-year electricity program at the age of 17, Hamerschlag performed fieldwork in Mexico and worked on an electrical plant on a Cuban sugar plantation. After graduation, he worked as an electrical and mechanical engineer in New York City.

Hamerschlag's path to becoming an expert in technical education began in earnest in 1892:

> The year 1892 found young Hamerschlag teaching mechanical drawing in the Hirsch School on Ninth Street

[New York], a position he relinquished to become associated with St. George's Evening Trade School. The rector of St. George's Church at that time, Dr. William S. Rainsford, was a pioneer in the institutional church movement, bringing his parishioners to the point of view that their responsibilities should include the rendering of service for the social and industrial as well as for the spiritual needs of the community. Shortly this church in Stuyvesant Square at Sixteenth Street on the East Side, a large and wealthy parish, was engaged in many welfare activities. Among them was a boys' club that started in 1891, with organized evening classes the next year in such subjects as typesetting, debating, stenography, drawing [and] carpentry [. . .].

The senior warden at St. George's in those days was John Pierpont Morgan [who purchased the Carnegie Steel Company in 1901, founding the United States Steel Corporation]. Morgan provided funds for the night school that, growing out of the club, was opened in 1892 in a narrow tenement house on East Eleventh Street, and which developed by 1902 to an enrollment of three hundred boys and occupied the whole of a five-story building at 505 East 16th Street. By virtue of his administrative ability, his understanding of the problems involved, and his leadership of under-privileged youth, Mr. Hamerschlag was appointed superintendent of this school at an early stage in its career. It was not long before he became consultant for the New York Evening Trade School, the Boys' Preparatory Trade School, New York, and the Highland Falls (N.Y.) Evening Trade School. (Tarbell, 28-29)

In addition to his success as a technical education specialist, Hamerschlag was highly regarded as an engineer in spite of his lack of formal engineering training. In 1898 in an invited speech before the American Institute of Electrical Engineers (now the Institute of Electrical and Electronics Engineers, IEEE), an organization that had awarded him a medal of excellence for research on cathode rays and induction coils, he bypassed the subject of engineering per se to instead present "The Education of Electrical Apprentices and Journeymen."

In his speech, Hamerschlag made the case for technical training for men to become electrical technicians whose skills at that time were

The Tartan

Andrew Carnegie and Arthur A. Hamerschlag on campus in 1910. General Photo Collection, Carnegie Mellon University Archives, Pittsburgh, Pennsylvania.

paramount for industrial expansion throughout the country. Apprentices were too few and far between and had no common training, and yet many jobs required men to work with their hands and have at least some technical training. That system had worked in other countries, and he felt that the middle ground of the technical school was imperative to the growth of American industry.

It was clear that in 1903, when a brand new technical school was being started in Pittsburgh, Hamerschlag was the right man for the job. He became director of this new endeavor. With some key decisions already made, it was now his responsibility to put it all together.

Initial Structure of the Carnegie Technical Schools

Hamerschlag agreed with the basic structure of the school that had already been determined by the trustees on the Carnegie Institute's Plan and Scope Committee. They had decided that the focus of the educational branch of Carnegie's institutional gift to Pittsburgh would be vocational training in science or art that went beyond high school but did not compete with the four-year degrees offered by existing Pennsylvania universities. In addition to day classes, a wide array of evening classes would be offered to allow those already employed to increase their earning potential. Course offerings would coincide with the needs of industry in the region, and only two-year certificates and three-year diplomas would be offered.

Four educational units—each having its own faculty, buildings, laboratories and shops—would make up what was now officially the Carnegie Technical Schools. They included The School of Fine and Applied Arts, The Margaret Morrison Carnegie School for Women (named after Carnegie's mother), and The School for Apprentices and Journeymen. But right from the start, the fourth unit, The School of Science and Technology, was the guts of the operation. It was divided into the School of Applied Design (architecture only) and the School of Applied Science (training draftsmen, foremen and engineers' assistants).

The School of Applied Science offered the most demanding set of courses and the most exacting admission standards. All first-year students took the same curriculum: English, economics, mathematics, physics, chemistry, drawing, and shop practice. Students then chose from six engineering fields known as "practices":

Chemistry practice included industrial chemistry and electro-chemistry.
Civil practice included structural design, railroad construction and municipal engineering.
Electrical practice included generation and transmission and electrical apparatus design.
Mechanical practice included machine design, prime movers and furnace and mill machinery.
Metallurgical practice included iron and steel manufacturing and non-ferrous metallurgy.
Mining practice included mine and quarry location and operation and smelting and refining.

Building Construction and Hiring

From the time Hamerschlag moved to Pittsburgh as director of the Carnegie Technical Schools, he was everywhere on campus. For much of his tenure, the campus was a loud, chaotic construction site. Because Andrew Carnegie seldom visited Pittsburgh by that time, Hamerschlag was his eyes, ears and hands from the beginning. It was probably not lost on Andrew Carnegie that Arthur A. Hamerschlag was only 31 when he accepted the position and would need all the energy he could muster.

Hamerschlag oversaw all of the initial building construction starting in 1903, working with Henry Hornbostel, the architect of the campus. Hamerschlag was involved in the hiring of carpenters, bricklayers and secretaries. Then he turned his attention to hiring the first faculty. The initial group consisted of 19 men and included architect Hornbostel and Hamerschlag himself. The new faculty—not all with college degrees—included engineers, scientists and architects. Hamerschlag also hired adjunct instructors to teach night classes. In addition to his position as a faculty member and director of the school, Hamerschlag was also the first dean of engineering.

The Carnegie Technical Schools would offer two-year certificates and three-year diplomas for day classes. Earning an engineering certificate in the evening program would require five years; nine years for an engineering diploma. (Evening enrollment eventually peaked in 1930 at almost 5,000 students.)

Electrical wiring, 1906. General Photo Collection, Carnegie Mellon University Archives, Pittsburgh, Pennsylvania.

Lecture room in physics, 1906. General Photo Collection, Carnegie Mellon University Archives, Pittsburgh, Pennsylvania.

Mechanical drawing, 1906. General Photo Collection, Carnegie Mellon University Archives, Pittsburgh, Pennsylvania.

Lecture room in electricity, 1906. General Photo Collection, Carnegie Mellon University Archives, Pittsburgh, Pennsylvania.

Class in surveying. General Photo Collection, Carnegie Mellon University Archives, Pittsburgh, Pennsylvania.

The first classes were held on October 16, 1905 in Industries Hall (now Porter Hall). On June 17, 1908, 58 "seniors" accepted diplomas, four in architecture and 54 in engineering. Their three-year degrees were the first awarded, and they would also be some of the last.

From Technical School to University

Despite Hamerschlag's intentions, it quickly became obvious that two- and three-year programs were not sufficient. Graduates were unable to compete with job applicants who had four-year degrees (even though Tech graduates felt that their training was equal or better). They could not join professional societies that were now starting to require at least a bachelor's degree for admittance. And graduates could not teach without a bachelor's degree.

Andrew Carnegie had said, "No school can be a creation but an evolution." So on April 20, 1912, the Carnegie Technical Schools added four-year bachelor degrees to its offerings and changed its name to Carnegie Institute of Technology.

This new era began by offering bachelor's of science degrees in chemical engineering, civil engineering, electrical engineering, mechanical engineering, metallurgical and mining engineering, architecture and, strangely enough, interior decoration. The first bachelor degrees (four of them) were awarded in 1915 in electrical, mechanical and metallurgical engineering. Each of these men had to have been "engaged in professional work consistent with his course for a period of not less than four years, and must have been in responsible charge of such work for not less than two years; in addition, he must present an acceptable thesis of not less than 5,000 words on some phase of his professional experience."

Also in 1912, 20 post-graduate students (men with degrees already from Carnegie Institute of Technology, Yale University, Dartmouth College, Pratt Institute and the Swiss Federal Polytechnic Institute) began as the first graduate students at the school now known as "Carnegie Tech," or simply "Tech." Held in the evenings only, these graduate courses in commercial engineering were geared toward men who were in the sales or production branches of engineering. Tech's first M.S. degree, an M.S. in physics, was awarded in 1914.

Not long after the first B.S. and M.S. degrees were issued, non-engineering faculty were consolidated into the Division of General Studies. That change showed early support for the Tech perspective that even engineers should receive a broad education, including humanities and cultural

John Hopkin Leete. General
Photo Collection, Carnegie Mellon
University Archives, Pittsburgh,
Pennsylvania.

John Hopkin Leete at left, Mr. and Mrs. Carnegie in the center, Arthur Hamerschlag top
row, right. General Photo Collection, Carnegie Mellon University Archives, Pittsburgh,
Pennsylvania.

26

courses. Now with a central faculty, a history class might include students from mechanical engineering, architecture and secretarial studies; faculty had to keep the attention of technical students in non-technical subjects. Tech was clearly on its way from a technical school to a full university but not without disruptions.

During World War I, Tech gave over its campus to the war effort. Using hastily built barracks and mess halls, up to 8,000 soldiers moved onto campus, marching and learning skills for jobs such as propeller maker, truck driver, band musician and electrician. Soldiers dug mock trenches, and engineers made a level drill field and parade ground out of the "cut," a deep valley that divided the campus. (Perhaps that's how today's "cut" got its name.) By the end of 1918, the soldiers and their temporary shelters were gone.

In 1919, Carnegie Tech's first doctoral degree was granted to Mao

Reserve Officers Training Corp., 1918. General Photo Collection, Carnegie Mellon University Archives, Pittsburgh, Pennsylvania.

Yisheng (then known as Thomson Eason Mao). Mao had received a bachelor's degree in 1916 in civil engineering from Tangshan Jiaotong University (now Southwest Jiaotong University) and an M.S. in civil engineering

Soldiers in front of Industries Hall (now Porter Hall), 1918. General Photo Collection, Carnegie Mellon University Archives, Pittsburgh, Pennsylvania.

at Cornell before coming to Tech. His dissertation: "Secondary Stresses in Bridge Trusses, Introducing the Graphic Method of Deformation Contour and Its Analytic Solution with Scientific Arrangement of Computations." A statue depicting Dr. Mao stands in an exterior alcove near Porter and Baker Halls.

As Tech matured, change was inevitable. Andrew Carnegie died on August 11, 1919 at the age of 83. His relationship with Hamerschlag had been one of trust and mutual respect. By June of 1922, Hamerschlag had retired from Tech. He felt that his job was done, and he wanted to work again as an engineer, which he did. He died just a few years later in New York at the age of 55.

The Langley Laboratory of Aeronautics was designed by Hornbostel and built in 1918 in 23 days in the location of what is now Hunt Library. While airplanes were not built there, airplane repair was taught in the building. Langley later became Skibo, the campus cafeteria and student center.

During Hamerschlag's tenure, Tech had evolved from a trade school serving local workers and industry into a university on par with other American technological universities. It was now time to build on that strong foundation, to smooth out the rough edges forged by bursts of rapid, sometimes frenetic growth. Once again some incredible people would guide the evolution of Tech, this time through the Depression, advances in education and another world war.

Langley Laboratory dedication, 1918. General Photo Collection, Carnegie Mellon University Archives, Pittsburgh, Pennsylvania.

Airplane repair was taught in Langley Laboratory of Aeronautics during World War I. General Photo Collection, Carnegie Mellon University Archives, Pittsburgh, Pennsylvania.

A Broader Perspective

A New Dimension for Carnegie Tech

President Baker. General Photo Collection, Carnegie Mellon University Archives, Pittsburgh, Pennsylvania.

Thomas Stockham Baker, Tech's second president (1922-1935), was the antithesis of Arthur A. Hamerschlag. He had served as music critic for *The Baltimore Sun* even as he was a lecturer of modern German literature at Johns Hopkins University, where he had received his Ph.D. Having spent time studying at German universities, he brought his international perspective to Tech in 1919 as vice president to Hamerschlag. Baker became president when Hamerschlag retired.

Baker coordinated campus beautification projects, increased emphasis on English requirements, and promoted the fine arts. He championed Tech to the local, national and world communities. He invited to campus executives from local companies whose employees took classes at Tech. Some companies, in turn, assigned "company deans" to coordinate their employees' classes, resulting in an increase in enrollment.

To enhance Tech's profile, Baker sponsored meetings of national organizations and brought famous scientists and engineers to campus for lecture series. He invited the public to an annual open house. Baker also led efforts to forge bonds with industry and government and to encourage collaborative research. His administration

Will you come to Dr. Baker's Christmas Party on Saturday afternoon, December the fifteenth from three to five o'clock in the building of the College of Fine Arts

PLEASE ANSWER

Invitation to President Baker's Christmas Party, 1934. General Photo Collection, Carnegie Mellon University Archives, Pittsburgh, Pennsylvania.

William Elton Mott. General Photo Collection, Carnegie Mellon University Archives, Pittsburgh, Pennsylvania.

broadened both the technical and social experiences of Tech students, and he helped to establish the strong applied research core that exists at CMU today.

Based on industry's needs and specific engineering challenges at that time, Baker and the dean of Engineering and Science, William Elton Mott, guided Tech toward research in coal and metals.

Beginnings of Interdisciplinary/Collaborative Research at Carnegie Tech

In 1923, because of Pittsburgh's unique position as a center for steel and aluminum companies, President Baker formed a Metallurgical Advisory Board to establish a metals research program on campus. The members of the board included presidents, general managers, or chief metallurgists of companies such as the Aluminum Company of America and the Molybdenum Company of America. Research on the production of metals was conducted collaboratively in the metals laboratory by metallurgists, physicists and chemists. This was the first example of what is now a long history of interdisciplinary research at Tech.

Previously, Hamerschlag had formed a Mining Advisory Board to help establish a mining and coal production research center. That had resulted in an ongoing relationship among the Department of Mining and Metallurgical Engineering, leading coal mine operators in Western Pennsylvania and the U.S. Government's Bureau of Mines. The U.S. Bureau of Mines had built its Central Experimental Station adjacent to Tech in 1917, having already begun work with the School of Applied Science.

To expand on those relationships and to promote Tech as a worldwide center of mining research, Baker instituted a series of three international

Coal research at Tech. General Photo Collection, Carnegie Mellon University Archives, Pittsburgh, Pennsylvania.

bituminous coal conferences on Tech's campus. President Baker traveled to Europe to encourage European governments to send their fuel experts. They did. From November 15-18, 1926, the first of three international coal conferences was held at Tech. More than 5,000 people attended, including many U.S. experts, and at least 20 foreign countries sent delegates, many representing their governments. Universities and industry sent researchers, and the globalization of the Carnegie Institute of Technology was underway.

Mechanical engineering students measure fuel consumption in the 1930s. General Photo Collection, Carnegie Mellon University Archives, Pittsburgh, Pennsylvania.

The success of the coal conferences resulted in the formation of the Carnegie Coal Research Laboratory in 1930 supported by the Buhl Foundation of Pittsburgh, General Electric (GE), Koppers, US Steel, New York Edison, Standard Oil and Westinghouse. This was among the first in a long line of research labs and centers at Tech with strong industry and government ties.

While Baker promoted work with industry, he also recognized the importance of strong research and a solid base in science. According to Baker:

> Engineering must have a background of pure science, if it is to advance; that the engineer is the liaison officer between the scientists' laboratory and the industrial plant; and that in enlarging the purely scientific resources of [Tech] the work of our own engineering faculty and students would not only be quickened, but it would secure wider recognition for the institution, as well as stimulate the intellectual and scientific life of Pittsburgh. (Tarbell, 113)

While Tech exploited its applied engineering skills, Baker recognized the need to advance science and technology research too. Under his

> Tech first used SAT scores in 1927 for admission into engineering and science.

administration, graduate instruction shifted from what had been an individual or tutorial basis to the beginnings of Tech as a research institution.

Never in good health, President Baker was finally unable to continue working by 1934 and resigned on September 17, 1935. He had broadened the foundation of Tech in many ways, including the introduction of applied research. Next in line for the presidency was an engineer whose relationship with one of the U.S.'s greatest scientists and engineers would launch Tech as a world-class research institution by changing the way students learn.

> Engineering enrollment, 1927-28: Day students 572, night students 856. Thirty-one percent of Tech students came from outside Pennsylvania.

Birth of the Carnegie Plan

Robert E. Doherty grew up in tiny Clay City, Illinois. In high school he built a "telegraph instrument" and, like Andrew Carnegie, worked as a telegraph operator. He felt that his small town education did not prepare him for college-level work, so he paid his own way for a year of prep school before starting at the University of Illinois in electrical engineering at the age of 21.

At Illinois he attended a lecture given by Charles Steinmetz. Steinmetz was a world-famous electrical engineer who worked at GE and who developed and invented several key technologies for motors and electric power, including the Law of Hysteresis, fundamental calculations for alternating current circuits, and the theory of electrical transients. Doherty was so inspired by Steinmetz that he joined GE when he graduated in 1918.

At GE, Steinmetz was equally impressed with Doherty's enthusiasm for learning, and he made Doherty his assistant. Steinmetz would eventually become like a second father to Doherty. Together, they created what became known as GE's Advanced Engineering Courses. Years later, the design of those courses would be instrumental in helping then-President Doherty shape the curriculum of Tech's engineering college.

Robert E. Doherty. Courtesy of the Museum of Innovation and Science, formerly the Schenectady Museum.

Charles Proteus Steinmetz

Born in 1865 in Breslau, Germany (now Wroclaw, Poland), Steinmetz was educated at the University of Breslau and the Swiss Federal Polytechnic Institute in Zurich, Switzerland, where he studied mathematics, electrical engineering and chemistry. He came to America in 1890 and worked for GE in Schenectady, New York, from 1892 to 1923 where he became head of the Calculating Department, which was responsible for much of the design work in the company. By 1894, he was Chief Consulting Engineer for GE. His work included multiphase motors, alternating current theory, and work with arc lamps and railway and fan motors.

He taught electrical engineering and electrophysics at Union College from 1902 to 1923 where he was chairman of the Electrical Engineering Department from 1902 to 1913. He served on the Schenectady Board of Education, including two terms as president.

He served as president of the American Institute of Electrical Engineers and vice president of what later became the IEEE. He was inducted into the National Inventors Hall of Fame in 1977.

General Electric's Advanced Engineering Courses

Other companies offered courses to their employees, but GE's Advanced Engineering Courses were different. While there were the usual lectures to explain theory and engineering concepts, open-ended problems were

assigned that taught the students how to apply their engineering knowledge and to collaborate on team projects to solve real-world problems.

The course was run by people who had taken it a year or two before. The course met usually half a day a week on company time. Employees worked collaboratively but also worked on problems at home.

Working with Steinmetz to design the GE courses, Doherty learned about problem solving and the professional responsibilities of an engineer. But he also learned what Steinmetz felt were the social responsibilities of the professional engineer: using problem-solving skills to become a productive member of a community. By example, while working at GE, Steinmetz was chair of Union College's Department of Engineering (1902-1914), a member of the Schenectady Board of Education and an officer in an organization called The National Association of Corporation Schools,

430 760 ADVANCED COURSE IN ENGINEERING CLASS '25A. FRONT ROW: R.E. DOHERTY, E.P. MILLER, H.A. WHITESEL, W.C. CAUTHEN, R.A. PLAUS, AF. SCHOEMANN, W.A. MOORE, L.P. SHILDNECK, R.S. ARTHUR, C.H. LINDER, C.A. WOODROW. BACK ROW: E.E. JOHNSON, G.W. ROBINSON, A.P. MACKERRAS, E.P. NELSON, R.M. RYAN, N.P. BAILEY, L.T. FOLSOM, H.J. HOFFMAN, D.D. COFFIN, A.S. GOULD, J.J. TAYLOR, R.W. BARR, K.C. MOBARRY. ABSENT MEMBERS: A.R. STEVENSON, JR., T.R. RHEA, E.W. VENNARD, B.L. ROBERTSON.
E320 6-27-25

Advanced Engineering Course at GE, 1925. Courtesy of the Museum of Innovation and Science, formerly the Schenectady Museum.

Advanced Engineering Course at GE, 1929. Courtesy of the Museum of Innovation and Science, formerly the Schenectady Museum.

a think tank consortium of companies looking for ways to educate their workers more productively. Steinmetz's concept of the combination of professional and social responsibility resonated with Doherty.

On October 26, 1923, Charles Steinmetz died. Doherty had just become GE's youngest consulting engineer, and he remained at the company for eight more years. As Doherty continued to teach the advanced engineering courses, he also continued to observe that new engineers coming into the company were not problem solvers. Something was lacking in engineering education.

In 1931, Doherty left GE for Yale to become head of the Electrical Engineering Department and two years later became Yale's dean of engineering. While there, he tried to broaden the engineering curriculum to include more problem solving and more humanities. But perhaps he felt that his new ideas didn't quite fit in with the established environment because in 1936, when he was offered the opportunity to come to Tech as its third president, he accepted.

Instead of immediately instituting radical changes, Doherty took his time, got familiar with the students, the campus, the curriculum and the culture. He must have been thrilled to be presiding over a fairly young and nimble institution that would allow him to implement what he felt was a proper engineering education.

Curriculum revision in engineering and science had begun at Tech in 1935 but was finalized after Doherty arrived. In Doherty's annual report of

ROBERT E. DOHERTY, M. S.
95 BRUCK STREET
SCOTIA, N. Y.

Oct. 28 '23.

My dear Mother:

I enclose the little
surprise which I referred to
in a letter to you recently.
How I wish Papa could know
it. I have thus reached the
goal I have been striving for;
and I now set out to make a
mark.

I have been congratulated
as "the youngest man who ever
bore the title of Consulting Engineer
in the General Elec Co".

But my heart is sad.
I feel somewhat as if I had
lost another father. I did not
realize how I loved Steinmetz
until I looked at him today
— for the last — and, as I stood
there, reviewed in rapid succession
the flashes of memory of what
he had done for me; what a
patient teacher and friend he
had been to me; how he had

38

inspired me to my best.
There he was. The greatest
mind of the age had left
us.

So it is a mixture of
joy and sadness. An odd
coincidence that the enclosed
announcement should have come
out on the very day Steinmetz
died — although it is dated few
days before.

We are all well. Billy
has been gaining half pound
a week (7 oz to be correct). My
throat is OK.

much love

Bob

Robert E. Doherty letter to his parents concerning the death of Steinmetz.
Courtesy of the Museum of Innovation and Science, formerly the Schenectady
Museum.

1937, curriculum revision—geared especially toward the College of Engineering—included the following: 1) reduced hours of class attendance, 2) emphasis on fundamental principles, 3) development of a desire to continue learning after graduation, 4) coordination of underlying science and mathematics and 5) inclusion of humanities and social sciences as related to professional work and citizenship responsibilities.

After trying various teaching methods over the next couple of years, it was finally decided in 1940 to divide engineering curricula into two branches:

> (1) Humanistic-Social. This would account for 20 percent of the students' time and would promote engineering with a social conscience, critical reading ability, logical thinking, effective writing, and the desire to continue to learn; and

> (2) Scientific-Technical. This would account for 80 percent of the student's time, focusing on fundamental principles and how they are derived, basic knowledge of specific fields of engineering study, application of knowledge and awareness of design and production costs, the ability to present engineering results, and a continuation of professional development.

GE/Yale/Tech Connections

Doherty had worked at GE, had been dean of Engineering at Yale, then came to Tech as president.

Benjamin Richard "Dick" Teare, Tech's dean of Engineering and Science from 1953 to 1965 had worked at GE from 1928 to 1933. In an IEEE interview, he explained: "The man who had set up the program at GE, . . . Robert E. Doherty, went to teaching and administration at Yale, and he offered me a job. And as an instructor at Yale, I taught undergraduate courses in problem solving, one at junior level and one at senior level. The students weren't in departments until their junior year. I also taught a similar graduate course. Some of this teaching was in partnership with Mr. Doherty, and some of it was on my own. The job was to teach basic problem solving, not new and fancier methods of problem solving."

Another Tech faculty member, Dennistoun Wood Ver Planck, had worked at GE from approximately 1929 to 1936. He also took the advanced engineering courses and eventually taught them. He became a Tech electrical engineering professor in 1946 and head of Mechanical Engineering beginning in 1947. He, too, taught at Yale (while working on his Ph.D. there) before coming to Tech.

Elliott Dunlap Smith had also taught at Yale while Doherty was there. Smith later became Tech's provost during Doherty's administration.

Even before Doherty arrived, during the 1930s the engineering and sciences faculty had pointed out the need for basic courses in physics and math, and the Educational Senate had voted to require more humanities courses for engineers. So faculty members were primed for change when Doherty arrived. Doherty felt that in order to increase teaching relevance, there should be a decrease in teaching load. In 1936, the teaching load was nine to 12 hours per week for full professors, some of whom also taught evening courses. By 1950, full professors' maximum teaching load was nine hours.

Tech students at Camp Davies, West Virginia, taking a surveying course in the summer of 1938. Courtesy of Linda Christiano Kramer. Her father, Nat Christiano, was a civil engineering student at Tech.

Tech students relaxing at Camp Davies, West Virginia, while attending a surveying course in the summer of 1938. Courtesy of Linda Christiano Kramer.

Tech students at the Blackwater Hotel in Davies, West Virginia, while attending a surveying course in the summer of 1938. Courtesy of Linda Christiano Kramer.

The Carnegie Plan

In 1948, after years of trial and error, Doherty's new way of teaching engineering—known broadly as liberal/professional education—became known specifically as the Carnegie Plan of Professional Education.

The plan included the Humanistic-Social and the Scientific-Technical branches of curriculum as laid out by Doherty in 1940, with the focus clearly on problem solving. The goal was to prepare engineering students to think and act as responsible engineers in their professional lives and also in their communities.

While formulated for use in engineering education, the concepts of problem solving and professional and social responsibility spread to Tech's sciences, humanities and even fine arts and business curricula.

Also in 1948, the Carnegie Corporation of New York sponsored the Inter-Professions Conference on Education for Professional Responsibility. It was chaired by Elliott Dunlap Smith, provost of Tech, and the board included Robert E. Doherty and faculty from Columbia, Harvard, New York University, University of Rochester, University of Chicago and Massachusetts Institute of Technology. Disciplines discussed included medicine, law, religion, business and engineering, and common teaching ground was sought. Because of President Doherty's Carnegie Plan, Tech was already considered as the example of engineering education excellence.

At the conference, Tech Professor Benjamin Richard Teare, Jr. presented a paper on professional engineering education in which he explained that the basic plan was to make the student do more of the work in the learning process, to have the teacher do less of his thinking for him, and to make less use of lectures, instructor-made illustrations, and routine exercises.

At that same conference, Provost Smith wrote about the Education of Professional Students for Citizenship, another aspect of the Carnegie Plan and a vestige of Steinmetz's influence on Doherty. He emphasized that humanities courses can be taught along with the technical curriculum so that students will develop a perspective as to how their professions fit into society.

Richard Drisko, George Westinghouse Scholarship holder, and Dr. Edwin L. Harder of Westinghouse Co. working on a transient analyzer at East Pittsburgh. September 13, 1946. General Photo Collection, Carnegie Mellon University Archives, Pittsburgh, Pennsylvania.

As the Carnegie Plan spread, many other institutions adopted aspects of the curriculum. What made it so successful at Tech was Tech's agile size (and concurrent ability to adapt) and the full participation of Tech faculty.

During the Doherty administration, full-time day enrollment increased as night school enrollment declined. As Tech struggled financially through the Depression, Doherty pushed to find more scholarship money.

Nuclear Engineering

Under the leadership of Tech's Physics Department, a synchro-cyclotron was built in the 1950s with funding from the Buhl Foundation, the Atomic Energy Commission, the Office of Naval Research and also from Tech. While problems plagued the design and construction, the synchro-cyclotron was ultimately built on 63 acres in Saxonburg. A Nuclear Engineering program was funded by $500,000 from Westinghouse Corporation. But by the 1970s, CIT chose not to continue with nuclear engineering and the program was discontinued.

A cooperative was set up with Westinghouse whereby students worked at Westinghouse for summers and for one full year during their undergraduate studies. That arrangement eventually shifted to conventional scholarships from Westinghouse. Other corporations stepping up to provide scholarships at that time included Koppers, Mesta Machine Co., Mine Safety Appliances Co., Pittsburgh Plate Glass (PPG) and US Steel Corp.

Magazines and newspapers circa 1949-1950 featuring the Carnegie Plan. General Photo Collection, Carnegie Mellon University Archives, Pittsburgh, Pennsylvania.

Graduate Research

Before Doherty's arrival, most graduate work at Tech was done on a tutorial basis or by coordinating projects involving both day and evening students. Doherty was determined to expand and strengthen graduate studies, and so he appointed John Christian Warner (chemistry professor and later Tech president) to the post of dean of Graduate Instruction.

Dr. E. C. Creutz, Physics Department; Dr. C. C. Monrad, head, Department of Chemical Engineering; Dr. R. E. Doherty; Dr. W. N. Jones, director, College of Engineering and Science; Dr. R. F. Mehl, head, Metallurgical Engineering Department; and Dr. J. C. Warner, head of the Chemistry Department. They are looking at plans for a synchrocyclotron and nuclear research laboratory. General Photo Collection, Carnegie Mellon University Archives, Pittsburgh, Pennsylvania.

During Doherty's administration, graduate enrollment increased from 45 to 369 students, with engineering and science students receiving more than three-quarters of the advanced degrees.

Research Funding

All faculty in all departments were encouraged to conduct research as Doherty pushed for increased funding from industry and private donations. His research objectives included balancing undergraduate and graduate instruction with research, integrating research into Tech's educational plan, promoting faculty based partly on research, and sharing research resources with industry.

In 1939, the Buhl Foundation donated $50,000 to develop a program of graduate study in electrical engineering. In 1943, Buhl followed up with $333,333 toward an electrical engineering professorship, and Benjamin Richard Teare, Jr. became the first chaired professor at Tech, the Buhl Professor of Electrical Engineering.

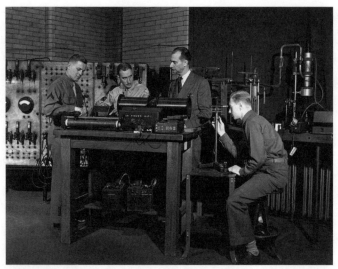

A physics experiment in the 1940s. General Photo Collection, Carnegie Mellon University Archives, Pittsburgh, Pennsylvania.

At the start of the Doherty administration, funding came mostly through foundation grants and totaled just $156,000 for the year. By 1950, funding from industry, government and from a research reserve fund built up during the war years, exceeded $1 million per year.

World War II

While the campus was again upended by wartime, the war effort created opportunities to expand government funding and research participation on campus. From 1940 to 1943, the Engineering Defense Program, financed through the Federal Security Agency of the Office of Education, brought students (mostly men, but also some women) to Tech to train them for employment in defense industries. Along with that program came money for equipment and labs, a welcome relief as labs were in sad shape after the Depression years.

In 1943, Army Specialized Training Programs were set up for basic engineering, advanced engineering and foreign language studies. This brought as many as 1,900 military personnel to campus but lasted for only 18 months. Westinghouse sponsored 40 to 50 women at Tech to study engineering. At least some of them worked as engineers at Westinghouse during the war.

Before the 1950s, the teaching of engineering involved worksheets and work-books. After the 1950s, labs were used.

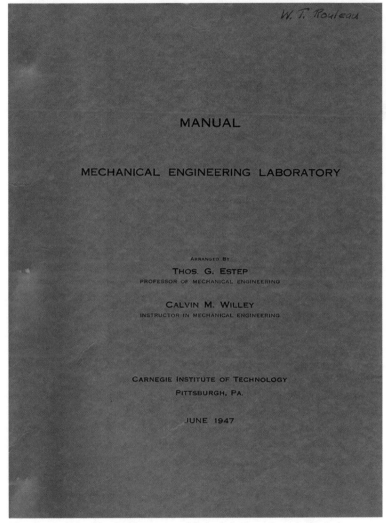

W. T. Rouleau

MANUAL

MECHANICAL ENGINEERING LABORATORY

Arranged By

THOS. G. ESTEP
PROFESSOR OF MECHANICAL ENGINEERING

CALVIN M. WILLEY
INSTRUCTOR IN MECHANICAL ENGINEERING

CARNEGIE INSTITUTE OF TECHNOLOGY
PITTSBURGH, PA.

JUNE 1947

The manual used by freshman mechanical engineering students in 1947. This manual belonged to Wil Rouleau who earned his B.S., M.S. and Ph.D. from Tech and went on to become a professor of mechanical engineering at Tech. As of today, long after his retirement, Professor Rouleau still occasionally spends time on campus. Courtesy of Wil Rouleau.

Engineering graduate students in 1936: 18
Engineering graduate students in 1950: 139

Students working on a York ice machine. This is the machine shown in the diagram from the 1947 mechanical engineering manual. Courtesy of Wil Rouleau.

The diagram of a York ice machine with engine dynomometer in the foreground, from the late 1920s. This is the machine whose diagram is shown in the 1947 mechanical engineering manual. According to Wil Rouleau, the photo was taken in the 1920s. "You can tell by the arc light fixture in the photo." Courtesy of Wil Rouleau.

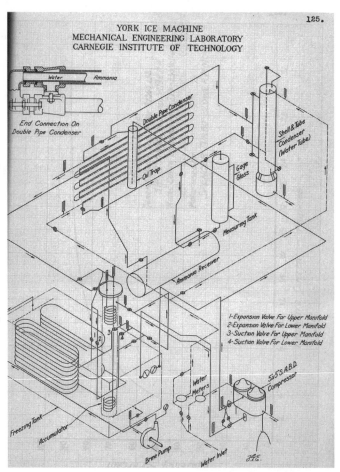

YORK ICE MACHINE
MECHANICAL ENGINEERING LABORATORY
CARNEGIE INSTITUTE OF TECHNOLOGY

125.

Water   Ammonia

End Connection On
Double Pipe Condenser

Double Pipe Condenser

Shell & Tube
Condenser
(Water-Tube)

Oil Trap

Gage
Glass

Measuring Tank

Ammonia Receiver

1-Expansion Valve For Upper Manifold
2-Expansion Valve For Lower Manifold
3-Suction Valve For Upper Manifold
4-Suction Valve For Lower Manifold

5x5 S.A.B.D.
Compressor

Water
Meters

Freezing Tank

Accumulator

Brine Pump

Water Inlet

Between 1943 and 1945, Tech enrollment plummeted as the Selective Service curtailed most deferments for engineering students. At the end of the war, however, veterans returned in record numbers. They brought with them maturity and academic focus, many of them picking up where their educations had been interrupted.

The Plan Lives On

With a broadened undergraduate curriculum, a vibrant and growing graduate program, and channels of research funding in place, Tech was poised for a bright future. Doherty retired in June of 1950, possibly knowing that he was ill, for he died suddenly a few months later. But the fundamental tenets of the Carnegie Plan were already firmly planted at Tech.

Like his predecessors, Doherty had helped to place the right people in positions to move Tech forward. That was especially true of the next president, John Christian Warner, who would continue Doherty's mission throughout the 1950s.

By the 1960s, a merger was in the works that would expand Tech's campus and provide the hope for long-needed financial stability. As to the engineering college, a shift occurred in leadership. Up to that point, the position of dean of engineering had sometimes been relegated to that of an intermediate-level administrator while the president led decision making in engineering, but not anymore.

Departments in the College of Engineering in 1936:
Chemical Engineering
    (including chemistry and general science)
Civil Engineering
Electrical Engineering
Management (commercial) Engineering
Mechanical Engineering
Metallurgical Engineering
Physics
Mechanics
Industrial Education
Printing
Enrollment: 1,160

Departments in the College of Engineering and Science in 1950:
Chemical Engineering
Chemistry
Civil Engineering
Electrical Engineering
Mathematics
Mechanical Engineering
Metallurgical Engineering
Physics
Enrollment: 1,719

Webster Newton Jones. General
Photo Collection, Carnegie Mellon
University Archives, Pittsburgh,
Pennsylvania.

Julia Randall Weertman.
From *The Thistle*, 1946.

Tech's First Female Student in Engineering and Science

In 1942, Julia Randall of the Mt. Lebanon neighborhood of Pittsburgh had
applied to Carnegie Tech's College of Engineering and Science, and she had
been rejected. She was ready to go somewhere else, but her father knew one
of Tech's faculty members. A meeting was arranged between Julia and Dean
Webster Newton Jones. "It was quite a long session," she recalled. "The dean
was skeptical that a woman could succeed in engineering and science. But it was
the war years, and most of the male students were gone. The dean reluctantly
accepted me as a student.

"At the time I started at Carnegie Tech, they were dropping the shop experience, which would have been great for me. They were replacing it with sociology
and social relations classes that to me were boring. I was not happy about that.
But our classes were very small, maybe only four or five students per class, and I
never met anything but kindness and encouragement from the faculty."

Julia received her B.S. in 1946, her M.S. in 1947 and her Ph.D. in 1951, all in physics, all from Carnegie Tech's College of Engineering and Science.

Julia met her husband, Johannes "Hans" Weertman, in her first year of graduate school. "He was a returning GI student in a physics class for which I was the
teaching assistant," she said. Now Julia Weertman, she went on to teach materials science at Northwestern and was inducted into the National Academy of
Engineering in 1988.

Although she officially retired in 1992 as the Walter P. Murphy Professor Emer-
ita of Materials Science and Engineering at Northwestern University, Julia continued working full time on research until the end of 2012. As of May of 2013, at the
age of 87, she still had one postdoctoral student.

An electrical engineering lab in the 1950s. General Photo Collection, Carnegie Mellon University Archives, Pittsburgh, Pennsylvania.

A metallurgy lab in the 1950s. General Photo Collection, Carnegie Mellon University Archives, Pittsburgh, Pennsylvania.

A Merger and a Separation

Doherty's successor, President John Christian Warner, had come to Tech in 1926. Trained in chemistry, Warner held many positions in both chemistry and engineering throughout the Doherty administration: head of the Chemistry Department, chairman of the Committee for Advanced Degrees in the College of Engineering and Science and dean of Graduate Studies in Engineering. In 1950, with so much of his career invested in Tech and as a champion of the Carnegie Plan, Warner was chosen to succeed Doherty.

Wil Rouleau, assistant professor in mechanical engineering, working with students on a lab assignment in 1951. General Photo Collection, Carnegie Mellon University Archives, Pittsburgh, Pennsylvania.

During Warner's presidency, the university's endowment grew and Tech finally got its own independent board of trustees. New buildings went up, including student housing and Hunt Library. Warner put in place an alliance with public schools for the teaching of advanced placement courses, and he increased faculty salaries. In addition to establishing the position of dean of Research, he also sought increased support for graduate fellowships, graduate scholarships and research assistantships.

Warner's choice for dean of engineering had to be a Doherty disciple. He found the right person, a man who focused the engineering curriculum on open-ended problem solving, who promoted acquiring or building the most forward-thinking engineering tools and who reached out to the global engineering community.

Benjamin Richard Teare

Benjamin Richard "Dick" Teare, Jr., the new dean of engineering, had been a GE/Yale colleague of Doherty's who had participated in the advanced engineering courses at GE, eventually becoming an instructor himself. In 1939, Teare had come to Tech as faculty in electrical engineering to build up a full-time graduate program in electrical engineering. He became department head of electrical engineering and dean of Graduate Studies before beginning as dean of the

Dick Teare portrait from Tech's yearbook, *The Thistle*

College of Engineering and Science in 1953. He was already a proponent of Doherty's liberal/professional educational environment.

In 1952, Teare had collaborated with another former GE/Yale/Doherty colleague, Dennistoun Wood Ver Planck, on a textbook entitled, *Engineering Analysis: an Introduction to Professional Method*. This textbook reinforced the tenets of the Carnegie Plan. It was written to develop an engineering student's "capacity to deal with situations that are new to him, by the application of fundamental principles, on his own initiative, and with well-ordered analytical thought processes." The course, described by Harold W. Paxton (Metallurgical Engineering and Materials Science [MMS], 1953 to 1994) consisted of

Freshman Year, 1950

In 1950, all engineering freshmen took the same classes. Their schedules consisted of two semesters each of chemistry, mathematics, English and history, a semester of engineering drawing and a semester of physics.

"open-ended problems in mechanical and electrical engineering consisting of a weekly set of conundrums, teaching how to look at problems."

In addition to this new approach to engineering education, a new tool had been developed that would forever change engineering: the computer.

In 1956, Tech's first computer, an IBM 650, arrived on campus. At that time, the Computation Center was being established through a joint project of the Graduate School of Industrial Administration, Psychology, Electrical Engineering and Mathematics. The budget for the first year was $53,000. In 1958, Tech became the first educational institution in the nation to offer computing courses for freshman engineering students.

Caricatures of civil engineering faculty, spring of 1956. Courtesy of Stan Over, civil engineering class of 1957.

Car "decal" placed on vehicles that toured the St. Lawrence Seaway the week before classes started in September of 1956. The project was led by Dr. D'Appolonia. Courtesy of Stan Over, Civil Engineering class of 1957.

The Internet's wide reach was still decades away, but Teare recognized at that time that another tool necessary for Tech's success was the establishment of a global engineering network.

Going Global

In the 1950s, Tech was beginning to expand its global presence. President Warner and Dean Teare spent a few weeks in Pakistan as consultants to an engineering school. Dean Teare traveled to Greece, Spain, Ireland, Liberia and Korea as an engineering educational consultant. He also worked with a representative from MIT to consult with a new Indian engineering school, the Indian Institute of Technology Kanpur (IIT). They helped to designate faculty willing to go there to help get the school started. Many U.S. engineers and engineering faculty members have attended IIT Kanpur, which is one of the top engineering schools in India today.

To expand further Tech's engineering influence outside the U.S., in 1957, Tech's new vice president for Development and Public Relations, H. Russell Bintzer, helped to organize a program that welcomed 600 Indian engineering graduate students to the U.S.

In 1956, during the second of a series of India's "Five Year Plans," the Indian government was developing and expanding the country's steel manufacturing industry. Approximately 2,000 Indian engineers needed further training outside of India. Some were scheduled to study in Germany, Great Britain, Australia and the USSR. The Ford Foundation felt that as many as possible of the engineers should be trained in the U.S., and so they helped to fund the Indian Steel Training and Educational Program (INSTEP).

INSTEP sponsored 600 graduate engineers to come for training in the U.S. Their orientation, work and school assignments, logistics and funding for the entire program was coordinated through Tech.

In six groups over four years, the men were brought to the U.S. via Pittsburgh and introduced to the culture. They were assigned to both universities and steel corporations in order to study in the classroom and in the workplace. After orientation, while some trainees stayed to study at Tech, others were assigned to schools such as the Illinois Institute of Technology, Lehigh University and Pomona College. They worked at

President Eisenhower with INSTEP students who were visiting Washington, D.C. General Photo Collection, Carnegie Mellon University Archives, Pittsburgh, Pennsylvania.

Dean Teare (front row, fourth from right) with Tech's last group of INSTEP students. General Photo Collection, Carnegie Mellon University Archives, Pittsburgh, Pennsylvania.

Bethlehem Steel, Inland Steel Company, Jones & Laughlin Steel Company, US Steel Co. and Weirton Steel Company, among others. By 1962, the men had returned to India to run the country's new nationalized steel industry, Hindustan Steel Ltd.

Engineering at Tech now had the beginnings of a global presence, a strong technical program, expanding research programs and a vision for the future. But the financial realities of supporting a growing institution forced a change on the university.

William W. Mullins. General Photo Collection, Carnegie Mellon University Archives, Pittsburgh, Pennsylvania.

William Wilson Mullins
Dean of Engineering and Science, 1966-1970

Mullins joined Tech in 1960 in the Department of Metallurgical Engineering (now Materials Science and Engineering). His short tenure as dean coincided with the upheaval caused by the merger of Tech and Mellon Institute. It was up to him to meet with Mellon Institute personnel and Tech faculty to help with the transition.

Adding to his already unenviable position, cutbacks in federal funding and the elimination of draft deferments for graduate students was causing a decline in graduate enrollment. At one point Dean Mullins said, "Since the history, tradition and reputation of the school is largely in its technical presence, we feel it would be a disaster to let it decline to mediocrity." While that did not happen, it illustrates what a frustrating time it must have been for the position of dean.

Mellon Institute + Carnegie Tech

As early as 1961, discussions of a merger had begun between the trustees of Tech and the trustees of the Mellon Institute.

The Mellon Institute had been founded in 1913 by Andrew and Richard B. Mellon as a research middle ground. The Mellons believed that the institute would fill the gap between basic university research and narrowly focused applied industrial research. The new endeavor was initially designated the "Mellon Institute of Industrial Research and School of Specific Industries of the University of Pittsburgh." It was funded by the Mellons and by industry-sponsored research.

Right away that arrangement did not please the University of Pittsburgh (Pitt) as researchers were not required to follow university protocol for degrees or funding, and Pitt did not acquire the increase in faculty that it had expected. Industry immediately demanded more of the researchers' time and more control over the publication of results. By 1928, the Mellon Institute had severed ties with Pitt and had become a nonprofit corporation.

By the 1950s, the Mellon Institute was struggling with its identity. While industry support had carried the institution for many years, more companies now had their own in-house research departments. The decision was made to shift focus to basic research, with the intention of securing substantial government funding. However, in 1965, the Mellon Institute was passed over for a Defense Advanced Research Projects Agency (DARPA) program on new materials that was hoped would secure its future as a center for basic research in materials science. In order to have any chance of obtaining government funding, the Mellon Institute would have to partner with an established university, and Tech was right next door.

The proposal to merge Mellon Institute with Tech was received in 1967 by what was then the H. Guyford Stever administration—President Warner having retired in 1965—and seemingly accepted at face value. Obvious benefits to Tech would be the Mellon Institute building itself, its endowment (an increase in Tech's endowment by 50 percent) and its labs, equipment and personnel. In addition, President Stever believed that a merger would easily complement the solid undergraduate program at Tech by making the university more attractive to prospective graduate students. He was right, and he was wrong.

The Mellon Institute building added acreage and facilities to the Tech campus, and the endowment helped to stabilize Tech's financial picture, at least in the short term. However, for the many individuals involved, this was an unhappy marriage of convenience.

Primarily, the merger overwhelmed Tech's Chemistry Department with assistant faculty, many of whom had chosen their careers based on *not* working in academia. It was years before the faculty situation settled out through resignations and retirements.

Up to the merger in 1967, engineering had been part of the College of Engineering and Science. By 1970, the newly named Carnegie Mellon University (CMU) had formed two separate colleges: an engineering college (all of the engineering disciplines) and the Mellon Institute of Science (chemistry, physics, computer science, biology and mathematics). Paying homage to the university's technical education roots, the engineering college took the name of Carnegie Institute of Technology (CIT).

The first dean of CIT was a man of unforgiving outspokenness. His goals for the college and his take-no-prisoners methods helped him lead engineering at Carnegie Mellon to new levels of achievement.

A Toor de Force

Herbert L. Toor had come to Carnegie Tech in 1953 as an assistant professor in Chemical Engineering. He received a B.S. from Drexel Institute of Technology and an M.S. and Ph.D. from Northwestern and had spent more than a year in the Navy during World War II. By 1967 he was head of the Chemical Engineering Department, after returning from an appointment of two years as a visiting United Nations Educational, Scientific and Cultural Organization (UNESCO) professor of chemical engineering in Madras, India. In 1970, he was chosen as the first dean of CIT.

Herb Toor. Courtesy of Beth Toor.

Toor's first order of business was funding. The existing faculty culture was to look at outside funding as, in his words, "rather vulgar." He prompted the "practical-minded engineers" in the newly formed CIT to realize that outside funding was critical, and they responded by increasing their pursuit of research funding. Three new centers emerged: Mechanical

Herbert L. Toor
Dean of Engineering, 1970-1979

Herb Toor grew up in Philadelphia, enlisting in the Navy at the age of 17 in 1944. He was discharged as a seaman first class shortly after the end of World War II. He obtained a B.S. degree in chemical engineering at Drexel in 1948 and an M.S. and Ph.D. at Northwestern, finishing in 1952.

Toor became assistant professor of chemical engineering at Carnegie Tech in 1953. He was promoted to associate professor in 1957 and to full professor in 1961. He became head of the Department of Chemical Engineering in 1967 and was appointed dean of the Carnegie Institute of Technology in 1970. In 1980, he became the first Mobay Professor of Chemical Engineering.

Author or co-author of more than 70 publications, Toor was awarded the Alan B. Colburn Award in 1964 by the American Institute of Chemical Engineers (AIChE). In 1990 he was elected to the National Academy of Engineering. In 2008, the AIChE named Toor one of the "One Hundred Engineers of the Modern Era" for his outstanding contributions in chemical engineering. He was also a fellow of the AIChE and of the American Association for the Advancement of Science (AAAS).

Toor retired in 1992 and was named professor emeritus at Carnegie Mellon. He died July 15, 2011 in Middlebury, Vermont.

Engineering's Processing Research Institute (PRI), the Center for Entrepreneurial Development (CED) and Materials Science's Center for the Joining of Materials (CJM).

Throughout his tenure in the 1970s, Toor usually got what he wanted but sometimes with unfortunate side effects related to his administrative style. In lieu of shirt and tie, he sometimes wore a T-shirt and sandals. He spoke like the sailor he had been, browbeating those he felt needed it. Some results of that were a loss of cooperation by industry executives he met who did not find his style deferential enough, and the resignation of department heads. Looking back years later:

> "It's pretty clear that I wasn't a *nice* dean at least with department heads. That becomes clear when I realize that the two deans I reported to as department head, Dick Teare and Bill Mullins, never put the kind of pressure on me that I put on the heads, and Dick and Bill were undoubtedly nice guys."

Nonetheless, he was relentless when he believed wholeheartedly in a cause. That pertained to his support for the recruitment of women and minority students and faculty.

Diversity

Many universities, including CMU, had been cited by the federal government in the 1960s as having a pattern of discrimination. Toor formed "Women of CMU," an organization of women at the university whose Women's Commission issued a Preliminary Report to the President in 1971. While it opened up a dialogue, it seems that not much progress was made.

However, in 1973, Toor hired Helen O'Bannon as assistant dean of engineering. Helen held economics degrees from Wellesley College and Stanford. She had done advanced economic research and analysis for several federal agencies in Washington in the 1960s. As assistant dean (and soon associate dean), she handled finances for CIT, and Toor asked her to take the lead in recruiting women for engineering and making CIT more attractive for women. The Faculty Senate voted her faculty status, a strong endorsement. She began a chapter of the Society of Women Engineers (SWE) and spoke to high school teachers and guidance counselors to encourage girls to study engineering. She went on to become the first woman commissioner on the Pennsylvania Public Utility Commission and a senior vice president at the University of Pennsylvania.

Already in place at Tech, beginning in 1963, was the Program to Aid Underprivileged High School Students, which by 1965 had become the School College Orientation Program of Pittsburgh (SCOPP). SCOPP merged with the national organization Upward Bound in 1966 (financed under the Economic Opportunity Act). Under this program, the Carnegie-Mellon Action Program (C-MAP), minority high school students attended summer programs at CMU in preparation for college-level work.

Toor supported C-MAP's vision and strove to do more. In an article in a CMU publication called *Focus* on April 5, 1977, he wrote:

Helen O'Bannon. Courtesy of the University of Pennsylvania Archives.

> Carnegie-Mellon's Affirmative Action Plan is the minimum that the law presently requires. . . . [The] goals for CIT are so low that the few women and minorities on the CIT faculty would be isolated and invisible to most students and faculty.

C-MAP

The Carnegie-Mellon Action Program (C-MAP) was established in 1968 to help disadvantaged minority students at the college level. Driven by a committee of faculty, staff and students after the university was approached by the Citizen's Committee of the Pittsburgh Community Action Program (CAP), the organization worked to admit and support black students at a time when racial tension threatened to derail opportunities for diversity in higher education. Please see Evolution of a National Research University by Ludwig F. Schaefer, pp. 45-53, for more about this organization.

In keeping with "CIT's stand in other areas where we set our sights (and perform) well above average and certainly well above minimum requirements," Toor pushed to increase women and minority enrollment in graduate programs so that those graduates could go on to faculty positions. For his efforts, Toor was nominated in 1982 for the Vincent Bendix Minorities in Engineering Award.

In 1970, CIT's existing departments of Chemical Engineering, Electrical Engineering, Mechanical Engineering, Civil Engineering and Metallurgy and Materials Science would be joined by a new engineering department, the first to be added since the founding of Carnegie Tech.

Engineering and Public Policy

In the late 1960s, William Wilson Mullins, then dean of engineering, asked engineering department heads to generate proposals for possible funding. E. M. "Rod" Williams, head of Electrical Engineering, proposed an undergraduate engineering program addressing the interaction between engineering and society. He called it "Sociotechnology," and he envisioned courses taught jointly by faculty from engineering and the College of Humanities and Social Sciences (H&SS). A seemingly radical idea being addressed at just a few other universities, it came at a time when American

Granger Morgan (right), head of Engineering and Public Policy (EPP), working with Baruch Fischhoff and Cynthia Atman on an influence diagram for use in designing a risk communication. General Photo Collection, Carnegie Mellon University Archives, Pittsburgh, Pennsylvania.

society was changing as evidenced by protests against the Vietnam War, a burgeoning environmental social consciousness and a rejection of the rigidity left over from the Cold War era.

In 1970, times were also changing at CMU. CIT was now a separate college, and in 1972, Richard M. Cyert, dean of CMU's Graduate School of Industrial Administration (GSIA), would become CMU's new president. Cyert believed in the Tech adage of pursuing excellence and being the first in new endeavors, and he supported this notion of cross-disciplinary study of engineering and its effects on society.

What Rod Williams had proposed as a partnership between CIT and H&SS ultimately became a collaboration between CIT and the School of Urban and Public Affairs (SUPA). Initially named Engineering and Public Affairs (EPA) to align with SUPA, this program began with labor-intensive interdisciplinary project courses, the first in 1970 conducted by Professors Toor, Chemical Engineering (ChE); Bob Dunlap, MMS (the first head of EPA); Dave Ragone, ChE; and graduate student Mike Massey (who would become the first joint Ph.D. in EPP). That project course examined airborne emissions in Pittsburgh and was conducted for the Allegheny County Air Pollution Control Variance Board. From there, the array of offerings grew.

SUPA

The School of Urban and Public Affairs at Carnegie Mellon (SUPA) began in 1970 through the efforts of R. K. Mellon, an influential businessman in Pittsburgh, Dick Cyert (dean of the Graduate School of Industrial Administration) and Carnegie Mellon professors William Cooper and Otto Davis. A graduate school charged with training business leaders to address the complex problems of urban communities, SUPA is now the Heinz College, renamed for Pennsylvania Senator H. John Heinz III who was killed in a plane crash in 1991.

Funding came initially from Ford Foundation funds held by Dean Toor, but the program was eventually supported by Alfred P. Sloan Foundation grants. The idea of examining the effects of engineering on society appealed to a number of the fairly young, untenured faculty in CIT, led by Bob Dunlap, with the full support of Gordon Lewis from SUPA and Bill Gouse, associate dean of both CIT and SUPA. By 1976, the program called EPA was not only thriving, it had become the Department of Engineering and Public Policy. How and why did it happen?

Department status for engineering and public policy would exemplify the Carnegie Mellon philosophy of being innovative and forward-thinking; the new department would champion the need, nationwide, to develop a community of professionals devoted to the problems of technology and society; and department status would aid in the recruitment of the best faculty and graduate students in the growing area of engineering and public policy.

Initially, the faculty senate opposed it, as did a fair number of CIT faculty. However, Toor had President Cyert's and Vice President Edward R. Schatz's support. In December of 1976, the Department of Engineering and Public Policy became the newest department in CIT.

Granger Morgan, who was recruited for a 50:50 joint appointment with the Electrical and Computer Engineering Department and given the charge of coordinating the development of an EPP graduate program, became the first head of EPP. Morgan recruited Indira Nair in 1978, and she subsequently became associate head in charge of the undergraduate program. The first Ph.D. awarded exclusively in EPP was to Alex Hills in 1979.

While EPP was an important first, it would be only one in a series of important firsts for CIT.

By the fall of 2012, doctoral enrollment in EPP would grow to 107.

Many Firsts

Design Beginnings

Up to this point, design was not taught in engineering education. The idea to start teaching design within CIT came, at least in part, from conversations between Herb Toor and Herbert A. Simon:

> After I [Herb Toor] became department head, we bought a house adjacent to the Schenley Park golf course and I frequently walked to the campus with Herb Simon whose path and time often coincided with mine. I found him a fascinating walking companion, full of interesting ideas and questions, and only long after we met did I find out that my fellow hiker was by then the famous Herb Simon who intimidated many people. But by then I had been talking and arguing with him too long to be intimidated.
>
> One day Herb said something like, "You engineers do a poor job of teaching design, and my book, *The Sciences of the Artificial* will show you how to improve things." I agreed about the problem; design, which is about synthesis, never fit well into the increasingly analytical present day engineering curricula and it was thought not to be scientific enough or researchable enough to be taken seriously. It was not taught happily by most faculty.
>
> If Herb [Simon]'s ideas could be put into practice, they would change how design was done as well as making it academically respectable. It would become intellectually interesting, researchable *and useful* to engineers, what should be the lodestar for academic engineers. *And* it offered us the rare opportunity to be first in a new area.

A committee, chaired by Steven Fenves, the new head of Civil Engineering, submitted a proposal for a Center for the Theory of Design to

Herb Simon in 1973. Addressing the drawbacks of the current piecemeal approach to teaching design in all branches of engineering, the committee proposed developing a solid, formal body of knowledge that was:

> (1) independent of the specific branch of engineering or technology involved, or, more precisely, included the degree of modeling or idealization required to represent a particular technology; and

> (2) equally applicable to describe a computer-aided or entirely manual design process as well as to specify a completely computerized process.

Herbert A. Simon

Often hailed as one of the most influential social scientists of the 20th century, Wisconsin native Herb Simon received his B.A. and later his Ph.D. in political science from the University of Chicago in 1943. After teaching for several years at the Illinois Institute of Technology, Simon began his career at CMU in 1949, as a professor and chairman of the Department of Industrial Management at Carnegie Tech.

Throughout his nearly 60-year career at CMU, Simon's expansive research fields included economics, sociology, cognitive science, psychology, computer science and political science. His research in decision making laid the groundwork for the development of artificial intelligence and won him the 1978 Nobel Prize in Economic Sciences for "his pioneering research into the decision-making process within economic organizations."

Simon was the recipient of many other awards and honors, including the A.M. Turing Award in Computer Science, the American Psychological Association Award for Outstanding Lifetime Contributions to Psychology, the American Society of Public Administration's Dwight Waldo Award, and the National Medal of Science. He authored nearly 1,000 scientific publications throughout his lifetime. He died in 2001 at the age of 84.

The proposed Design Research Center (DRC) would be dedicated to the improvement of the quality and diversity of computer aids for all phases of engineering design and across all engineering and allied design disciplines, with particular attention to computer aids applicable in the early conceptual stages of design.

Physical space would have to be found on campus for the DRC, and participation from Computer Science (CS) would complement initial faculty from Civil, Chemical, Electrical and Mechanical Engineering, who would have joint appointments. A computer—a PDP-10 processor—was purchased. Fenves believed the proposed three-year budget for faculty

Arthur W. Westerberg
Art Westerberg received his B.S. at the University of Minnesota in 1960, his M.S. at Princeton in 1961, and his Ph.D. from Imperial College, University of London, England in 1964. Prior to coming to CMU in 1976, he spent two years as a senior analyst at Control Data Corporation and nine years as a faculty member in Chemical Engineering at the University of Florida.

He was director of the Design Research Center from 1978 to 1980, head of Chemical Engineering from 1980 to 1983 and founding director of the Engineering Design Research Center. Westerberg has more than 170 publications in process flowsheets and information and computer technology-based tools to support collaboration among diverse design teams. He has received many awards, and he became the John E. Swearingen Professor of Chemical Engineering at CMU in 1982. He became a member of the National Academy of Engineering in 1987.

Westerberg retired in June of 2004.

Arthur W. Westerberg. Courtesy of Department of Chemical Engineering.

(four proposed), graduate students (eight initially), administration and computer maintenance, and for the initial investment in office space, would be an "enormous" $900,000.

The center was funded in 1974, but it was greatly scaled back, using $50,000 from the Ford Foundation to support two small offices, a secretary and the partial salary of a director. During that time, Fenves attended a NATO workshop where he met two future faculty members, both proponents of design: Steve Director and Art Westerberg. Eventually they both joined CMU, Steve in Electrical Engineering, and Art in Chemical Engineering. At a follow-up workshop, the three of them met Gary Powers, a chemical engineer, who was recruited to CMU and eventually became the first director of the DRC.

From 1974 to 1980, the emphasis within the DRC was to move beyond the jargon of the respective disciplines in order to transpose design methods from one discipline to the others. According to Angel G. Jordan, dean of engineering

March 13, 1973 memo from Toor to Cyert regarding the Theory of Design:

"I want to start moving on the Theory of Design. Operationally, this means I would like to start looking for faculty in this area—perhaps three for next year with a commitment to expand along the lines discussed in the CIT planning documents.

"I realize this is a gamble as far as funds are concerned, but this is just too hot a subject to play conservatively. Let's gamble!"

from 1979 to 1983, the DRC was a "loose federa-
tion of twenty-five or so faculty and graduate
students from engineering, architecture, computer science, design, mathematics, GSIA and
SUPA. They participated in monthly meetings,
lunches, research projects (co-directed by at least
two faculty from different departments) and a
few jointly taught courses."

Between 1980 and 1985, support for the
DRC came from the Alfred P. Sloan Foundation
and the Sun Company. In 1984, the National Science Foundation (NSF) had put out a call for
proposals for engineering research centers with
an opportunity for funding of up to $20 million.
Requirements included emphasis on interdisci-

Steven Fenves.
General Photo
Collection, Carnegie
Mellon University
Archives, Pittsburgh,
Pennsylvania.

plinary research and a commitment of at least 10 percent of an institution's graduate engineering students. The first CIT proposal was not funded, but the second pass, submitted in 1986 by Granger Morgan, Art Westerberg, Steven Fenves and Steve Director was funded by the NSF. Art Westerberg became director as the DRC became the Engineering Design Research Center (EDRC). The Center ultimately received more than $27 million over 11 years.

Engineering Design Research Center (EDRC)

Angel G. Jordan. General Photo Collection, Carnegie Mellon University Archives, Pittsburgh, Pennsylvania.

The broad goal of the EDRC was to play a leadership role in developing and integrating concepts and methodologies that would allow U.S. industry to design better products more quickly. More specific goals included:

> (1) making a significant contribution to design science in the form of methodologies, computational tools and environments for engineering design;

(2) educating a new generation of engineering design practitioners, educators and researchers for industry and academia;

(3) infusing the engineering curriculum with engineering design textbooks and other course materials; and

(4) collaborating with industry to support improved design practice by exchanging knowledge, people and software tools.

The EDRC produced improved design tools in areas such as optimization and design synthesis. Research within the center led to the transition of tools and concepts across multiple disciplines. Over the 11 years of its existence, the EDRC supported 116 M.S./M.E. students and 142 Ph.D. students.

Disciplines and colleges at CMU involved in the EDRC:
Chemical Engineering
Electrical and Computer Engineering
Materials Science
Civil Engineering
School of Computer Science
Robotics Institute
Architecture
Graduate School of Industrial Administration
Design Department of the College of Fine Arts
The Heinz School

While the EDRC was CIT's first NSF engineering research systems center, an unprecedented second one would follow.

Strategic Faculty Hires between 1974 and 1984

The success of the EDRC was due in part to a concerted effort in the 1970s and early 1980s to go out and find the most qualified faculty candidates in emerging research areas. This effort was led by President Cyert. When he became president in 1972, Cyert met with all of the engineering department heads about hiring. Because they had not been looking nationally for potential faculty, he told them

Robotics Institute
In 1979, Professors Raj Reddy (CS) and Angel Jordan (ECE) and Westinghouse Electric Corporation president Tom Murrin founded the Robotics Institute with the goal of making it the best place on the planet to do robotics research. When Jordan became dean in 1980, he made the controversial decision to place the Robotics Institute within computer science rather than engineering. Ultimately, CS became a separate school, and the Robotics Institute became a unit within CS and continues to collaborate with faculty and students from CIT.

James C. Williams. From *The Thistle*, 1985.

that from that time on, they were required to do a national search.

Because of that change in attitude, Steve Fenves (Civil Engineering), Steve Director (Electrical Engineering), Art Westerberg (Chemical Engineering), Ron Rohrer (Electrical Engineering), Sarosh Talukdar (Electrical Engineering) and Gary Powers (Chemical Engineering) were recruited for their connection to design. Other important hires included Granger Morgan (Chemical Engineering and eventually Engineering and Public Policy), John L. Anderson (Chemical Engineering), Jim Williams (Metallurgical Engineering and Materials Science) and Ignacio Grossmann (Chemical Engineering). Mark Kryder (Electrical and Computer Engineering), an expert in magnetics, was recruited to CIT in 1978. He led the formation of what would become CIT's second NSF engineering research center.

The Data Storage Systems Center

According to Kryder, in April of 1982, the mission of what would become the Magnetics Technology Center was formulated based on discussions with 20 outstanding industry people who were experts in magnetics technology. Approximately 30 topics in magnetics storage research were deemed suitable for Ph.D. theses topics, and IBM and 3M funded the center. As to CMU's commitment, a cleanroom was built in Hamerschlag Hall.

In 1989, with the hope of expanding the Magnetics Technology Center, a proposal was submitted to NSF for an engineering research center. No university had ever received simultaneous funding for two NSF engineering research centers. Nonetheless, NSF awarded the proposal in 1990, and the Magnetics Technology Center became the Data Storage Systems Center (DSSC). Between 1990 and 2001, with funding of more than $100 million, the DSSC was the preeminent university-based research center of its kind in the world.

The original long-term goal of the DSSC was to accelerate the rate of progress in data storage device density and performance by establishing a long-term research and education program with

Paul Christiano. General Photo Collection, Carnegie Mellon University Archives, Pittsburgh, Pennsylvania.

thrusts in magnetics, magneto-optics and allied technologies such as signal processing and coding, with a target of increasing storage density by several orders of magnitude beyond the capabilities at that time. According to Mark Kryder, "At the time the DSSC was funded, the areal density on disk drives was about 100 megabits per square inch and increasing at approximately 25 percent per year. By 2001, the areal density growth rate had exceeded 100 percent per year and an areal density of 100 gigabits per square inch had been demonstrated."

Steve Director; Professor Dan Siewiorek, ECE and CS; Larry Sumney, president and CEO of the SRC. Courtesy of ECE Department.

Today the DSSC, now fully funded by industry, is an interdisciplinary research and educational organization where faculty, students and researchers from a broad array of academic disciplines collaborate in pioneering theory and experimental research that will lead to the next generation of information storage technology.

The SRC-CMU Computer-Aided Design Center

As the Magnetics Technology Center was being founded, the Electrical Engineering Department had been renamed the Electrical and Computer Engineering Department (ECE). Within the field of electrical and computer engineering, a new organization had just been formed to match university research with industry need. That organization was the Semiconductor Research Corporation (SRC):

> In the late 1970s and into the next decade, the American semiconductor industry had been witnessing a rapid erosion of its technological leadership. In an environment of accelerating change, complexity and cost, the burden of

75

maintaining duplicative company-based research laboratories had become unsustainable.

Founded in 1982 by the Semiconductor Industry Association to implement an innovative form of industry-university cooperation in research related to semiconductor devices, the SRC, by 2000, had invested over one-half billion dollars in semiconductor research in U.S. universities. Well over 1,000 graduate students had participated by that time, gaining highly relevant experience. Most went to work in U.S. semiconductor companies. (www.src.org)

In 1982, one of the first SRC centers of excellence was awarded to the ECE Department at CMU. Of the three inaugural centers, CMU and the University of California, Berkeley received funding for Centers of Excellence in Computer-Aided Design while Cornell received funding for a Center of Excellence in Microscience and Technology. Steve Director, ECE Department head at the time and later dean of CIT, served as the

Steve Director. Courtesy of ECE Department.

Stephen W. Director
Dean of Engineering, 1991-1996

Director grew up on Long Island, New York, and received his B.S. from the State University of New York at Stony Brook in 1965. He went on to earn a Ph.D. in electrical engineering from the University of California at Berkeley in 1968. He taught in the Electrical Engineering Department at the University of Florida, Gainesville and served as a visiting scientist at IBM's T.J. Watson Research Center before arriving at CMU in 1977.

At CMU, Director served as the head of the Department of Electrical and Computer Engineering (1982-1991) and dean of the College of Engineering (1991-1996). During that time, he also founded the SRC-CMU Research Center for Computer-Aided Design, which he directed from 1982-1989. After leaving CMU in 1996, Director went on to serve as the dean of the College of Engineering at the University of Michigan, provost at Drexel University and provost and senior vice president of Academic Affairs at Northeastern University.

Director has served as president of the Institute of Electrical and Electronic Engineers Circuits and Systems Society, is a fellow of the IEEE and of the American Society for Engineering Education and is a member of the National Academy of Engineering. In addition to serving on several boards and committees, Director is also the author of over 150 scientific papers for which he has received numerous awards and recognitions.

director of what was then known as CMU's Center for Electronic Design Automation (CEDA) from 1982 to 1989.

Director established an industrial affiliates program that augmented funding from the SRC. By 2000, CEDA was receiving significant funding from other agencies such as the NSF and DARPA. As computer-aided design (CAD) matured, research in the center began to shift more toward design methodologies and design of actual integrated electronic systems. This shift in focus was the impetus for CEDA to evolve into the Center for Silicon System Implementation (CSSI), which melded the strong CAD algorithms research with the expanded focus on design methodologies and circuit design.

By the late 1980s, a change in curriculum was on the horizon for CIT. It would alter the framework of undergraduate engineering education at CMU.

A Fresh Look at CIT's Freshman Curriculum

Ever since the introduction of the Carnegie Plan, adopting the best methods to teach engineering within CIT had always been a prime concern. In 1990, Dean Christiano felt that it was time to look closely at the structure of the freshman year curricula. He initiated discussions with all CIT departments asking them for their feedback. The result of those discussions was a significant alteration of the freshman year throughout the college.

To expose students to real engineering right from the start, beginning in 1991, all incoming CIT freshmen were required to choose two out of six possible introduction to engineering classes (metallurgical engineering and materials science, mechanical engineering, engineering and public policy, electrical and computer engineering, civil engineering or chemical engineering). Similar to the GE Advanced Engineering courses taught decades earlier, these courses would provide hands-on engineering experience and a context for related courses in science and mathematics. They would introduce the students to the range of engineering practices and to methods for engineering design and problem solving. Because these new courses were 12 units, the number of required freshman courses was dropped from five to four.

While the number of humanities and social science courses remained at a total of eight, the options to choose from were expanded.

A series of designated engineering minors were introduced. They included automation and control, biomedical engineering, engineering design, environmental engineering, electronic materials, and manufacturing engineering. Each minor required seven to eight courses with the expectation of some interdisciplinary exposure.

As all departments within CIT were incorporating changes to the freshman year, ECE used this as an opportunity to "wipe the slate clean," essentially changing its entire curriculum.

Wipe the Slate Clean

In January of 1990, ECE Department head Steve Director put together a committee within ECE called "Wipe the Slate Clean." Looking beyond just the freshman year, this committee reevaluated the entire ECE curriculum. The committee started by ignoring the rules set forth by ABET (the Accreditation Board for Engineering and Technology, Inc.) so that committee members could suggest any options, no matter how radical. The result of their work was a new model of undergraduate engineering education.

Why was a reevaluation of the ECE curriculum necessary?

> (1) It was becoming difficult to fit all course requirements and new subjects into a four-year degree program. Ever increasing amounts of material were being included in each 12-unit class requiring more than 12 hours per week of students' time. The result was that information was not being understood at a deep enough level.

> (2) Students weren't able to see how topics fit together because of disjointed course offerings, causing some excellent students to change majors or drop out.

> (3) Few students had actual lab or technical skills like those taught initially at Carnegie Tech.

> (4) Knowledge gaps existed among incoming students. Some students were struggling because their high school courses had not been rigorous enough. Many students didn't understand underlying fundamentals, even if they had gotten good grades in high school.

What had been electrical engineering for so long now included a broad and ever-expanding spectrum of topics and disciplines. The committee recognized that it was no longer possible for students to learn about every aspect of electrical and computer engineering. They decided that the curriculum should be based more on topics than on course subjects. The key to the new curriculum would be flexibility.

Some of the changes included greatly reducing the number of core courses and replacing them with course requirements in breadth areas. The breadth areas chosen were physics, signals and systems, circuits, computer software (with some courses being taken in the School of Computer Science) and computer hardware.

John L. Anderson. Courtesy of John L. Anderson.

Electrical and Chemical Engineering students would no longer have to achieve basic mastery in every area. With the flexibility to follow a unique path, students could now choose breadth or depth; they could take both EE and CE courses or concentrate on a specific topic. Those needing more preparation time for specific engineering courses could postpone them until later in their schedules. The number of free electives was greatly increased.

As with the Carnegie Plan decades before, this new curriculum was widely discussed outside of CMU. The reasons for reevaluating the curriculum where not unique to CIT; other engineering colleges were also facing the same types of issues with their own students.

The ABET Task Force agreed that flexibility and innovation in engineering education was crucial to attract, retain and prepare students for careers in engineering. ABET accreditation was received in 1991 for this radical engineering curriculum, opening the door for others to follow. Several hundred copies of the new curriculum design document were requested by colleagues around the world. When Steve Director became dean in 1992, he encouraged the other CIT departments to adopt the ECE style of curriculum, which they did.

The Information Networking Institute

In 1989, during the transition from Dean Williams to Dean Christiano, the Information Networking Institute (INI) was founded. This was the nation's first research and education center devoted to information networking. It grew out of a need of EPP faculty who were working on telecommunication policy. EPP's Marvin Sirbu designed the first curriculum and EPP Ph.D. Alex Hills returned to campus to become the first director. In 2000, INI became part of CIT.

The INI was a perfect example of cross-discipline collaboration. INI programs combined coursework from several CIT departments and also from the School of Computer Science, the Tepper School of Business and

The Department of Civil Engineering Becomes the Department of Civil and Environmental Engineering.

In the 1970s, the public was becoming more concerned about energy conservation and maintaining and improving the quality of the environment. At that time, the Department of Civil Engineering (CE) began adding faculty who specialized in these areas.

On April 22, 1994—Earth Day—the Department of Civil Engineering became the Department of Civil and Environmental Engineering (CEE). Dick Luthy, head of the Civil Engineering Department at the time explained:

"It was both a change that has naturally evolved over the last 25 years as well as a return to one of civil engineering's roots.

"Beginning about 100 years ago, specialists in civil engineering, known as 'sanitary engineers,' were called upon to design processes and products to respond to society's needs, such as water filtration systems to save people from devastating health problems. Today our program is directed toward fundamental understanding of both natural environmental systems and engineered processes. Our graduates are trained to think about the impacts of human activity and the design and deployment of technology."

the Heinz College. It would eventually partner internationally with Athens Information Technology in Greece, the University of Hyogo in Japan and Carnegie Mellon Portugal, and it would offer bicoastal programs in collaboration with Carnegie Mellon Silicon Valley.

The Department of Biomedical Engineering

As in information networking, CIT recognized early the need for collaboration in another emerging research area, this time in biotechnology. In 1967, biotechnology had begun as a program at CMU, offering a minor in undergraduate biomedical engineering. Limited by CMU's lack of a medical school, the Carnegie Mellon Department of Biological Sciences formed a joint program in 1983 with the School of Medicine at the University of Pittsburgh to offer an M.D./Ph.D. program.

In 2002, the Biomedical Engineering Department was officially established within CIT. It leveraged extensive collaborations with researchers and physicians from the University of Pittsburgh Medical Center, the Western Pennsylvania/Allegheny General Hospital System and the Children's Hospital System in Pittsburgh.

Undergraduate students who elected biomedical engineering as a major also had to declare a major in one of the traditional engineering disciplines of chemical engineering, civil engineering, electrical and computer engineering, materials science and engineering, or mechanical engineering. Graduate programs included

National Rankings
According to the *U.S. News and World Report* rankings of America's Best Colleges, in 1996, undergraduate engineering in CIT was ranked 3rd in the country while graduate engineering was ranked 6th where it remained in 2012. Undergraduate engineering was ranked eighth and had never dropped out of the top 10.

a master's in biomedical engineering, an M.D./Ph.D. in collaboration with the University of Pittsburgh School of Medicine and a Ph.D. in biomedical engineering. The Department of Biomedical Engineering would eventually find itself in a new state-of-the-art home, thanks in large part to CIT's next dean.

As the 21st century began, CIT was poised for leadership in fields of study barely imagined just a few years before. It was also exporting its expertise and resources across the globe.

Full Steam Ahead for the Little Engineering College That Could

Exploiting Expertise in a Collaborative Environment

In 1996, funding for the EDRC was expiring. At that time, Dean John L. Anderson met with Art Westerberg, Steven Fenves, Dan Sieworek and the EDRC's executive director, Georgette Demes, to discuss possible funding sources to allow for continued design research. Demes proposed an alliance with Lehigh University's Center for Advanced Technology for Large Structural Systems (ATLSS). If funding from Pennsylvania could be obtained, the two universities would work together to aid Pennsylvania-based industry. The Pennsylvania Infrastructure Technology Alliance (PITA) was born when the Commonwealth of Pennsylvania supplied funding of $2.5 million a year for five years. The goal was to develop technological innovations for the improved economic growth and efficiency of Commonwealth companies and agencies.

That financial support for PITA kept engineering design research alive at CMU and led to the creation of the Institute for Complex Engineering Systems (ICES) in 1997, whose first director was Pradeep Khosla.

Programs within ICES were charged with extending the collaborative work accomplished through the EDRC and targeting unexploited synergies within CIT. The 2012 budget for ICES was $8 million.

In 2003, as a result of the attacks on the World Trade Center on September 11, 2001, research on security conducted within ICES led to the creation of CyLab, one of the largest university-based cybersecurity research and education centers in the U.S.

CyLab was an NSF CyberTrust Center affiliated with the Computer Emergency Response Team (CERT) at the Software Engineering Institute. More than 50 faculty and 100 graduate students from ECE, EPP and six other departments and colleges across CMU worked through CyLab establishing relationships with organizations, companies or research laboratories within companies through a formal corporate partnership program.

Corporations could leverage CyLab's substantial existing support from Carnegie Mellon University and external sponsors.

CyLab has offered programs in Greece and Korea. Currently CyLab Japan (in collaboration with Hyogo Prefecture) offers a master of science degree in information networking (MSIN) through the Information Networking Institute.

Taking advantage of the expertise and collaborative environment on campus, other cross-disciplinary centers were formed to address particular needs. Examples include the Masters of Product Development program (Mechanical Engineering, the School of Design and the Tepper School of Business), Computational Materials (CIT and the Mellon College of Science), Sensed Critical Infrastructure (now the Pennsylvania Smart Infrastructure Incubator) (CIT and the School of Computer Science), Nanotechnology, Air Quality and WaterQUEST (Water Quality in Urban Environmental Systems) (CIT and Mellon College of Science) and Mobility (CyLab and CMU Silicon Valley).

One of the larger collaborative efforts is the Center for Implantable Medical Microsystems (CIMM) that brings together faculty members and students from CIT, Mellon College of Science and the Tepper School of Business. CIMM's mission is: 1) to develop "near-zero invasive" implantable diagnostic monitors and therapeutic tools by merging a range of microsystem technologies; 2) to develop modular technologies that enable rapid design of these implantable microsystems for specific applications; and 3) to partner with physicians to drive design, implementation and clinical studies of implantable microsystems.

The CIMM's aim is to solve unmet medical needs and improve outcomes for a multitude of medical conditions such as cancer, HIV, epilepsy and spinal cord injury.

Extending beyond campus, the Institute of Advanced Energy Studies (IAES) is a collaborative effort among CMU, Pitt, West Virginia University, Penn State and Virginia Tech and the Department of Energy's National Energy Technology Laboratory. The IAES was initially funded at $20 million over three years and was renewed in 2010 at $60 million over five years.

Global Expansion of the CIT Brand

In 2004, Pradeep Khosla became dean of CIT. Already known never to accept "no" for an answer, Khosla immediately began to build on the strengths of CIT, strengths that included emphasis on cross-collaboration, vigilance in the teaching of engineering, and inclusion in the global engineering community. CIT began branching out by establishing a physical presence in Portugal, China and Rwanda.

In October of 2006, Professor José M. F. Moura (ECE and Biomedical Engineering) was instrumental in the creation of the Information Communication Technologies Institute (ICTI), a partnership between Carnegie Mellon University, nine universities in Portugal, four Portuguese research

---

Pradeep K. Khosla
Dean of Engineering, 2004-2012

Khosla received his B.A. in technology from the Indian Institute of Technology in Kharagpur in 1980 and went on to earn his M.A. and Ph.D. in electrical and computer engineering from CMU in 1984 and 1986, respectively. He then began teaching at CMU where he held several esteemed positions, including University Professor, founding director of the CMU CyLab, head of the Department of Electrical and Computer Engineering, director of the Information Networking Institute and founding director of ICES. In 2004, he was named dean of the College of Engineering, a position he held until 2012.

Khosla has authored over 350 scientific publications. His research in areas such as embedded software, intelligent systems and cybersecurity has resulted in numerous awards and honors, including the George Westinghouse Award for Education (1999), the SiliconIndia Leadership Award for Excellence in Academics and Technology (2000) and a Lifetime Achievement Award from the American Society of Mechanical Engineers (2009).

In the fall of 2012, he began his new role as chancellor of the University of California, San Diego.

---

institutes, Instituto de Soldadura e Qualidade and several companies in Portugal. This program was financed by the Portuguese government and Portuguese industries.

The ICTI supports research projects and offers professional M.S. programs and Ph.D. education in traditional areas such as electrical and computer engineering and computer science, but also in information networking and security, software engineering, cyber-physical systems, human-computer interaction, engineering and public policy, applied mathematics, and technology innovation and entrepreneurship with a focus on information and communication technologies.

Pradeep Khosla. Photo by Najib Joe Hakim.

Students receive dual M.S. degrees or dual Ph.D. degrees, one from CMU and one from the Portuguese university where they study, putting them in a position to become leaders in their fields.

In addition to faculty involvement from CIT, the ICTI also includes participation from the School of Computer Science, the Dietrich College of Humanities and Social Sciences (formerly H&SS), the Tepper School of Business and the Heinz School of Public Policy and Management.

Starting in the fall of 2012, classes for graduate education and research began in Kigali, Rwanda, at the Carnegie Mellon-Rwanda Center for Excellence for Information and Communication Technologies.

CIT formed a joint venture with Sun Yat-sen University (SYSU-CMU) in China's Guangdong Province, for undergraduate and graduate education and research. The first class is scheduled for the fall of 2013.

Also in 2013, CMU will partner with India's Shiv Nadar University (SNU), a newly formed technology university, for a dual-degree undergraduate engineering program. It will include either a B.S. in electrical and computer engineering or mechanical engineering and a bachelor of technology degree from SNU.

Expanding a little closer to home, the Carnegie Mellon Silicon Valley campus that had been established in 2002 as a satellite to the School of Computer Science became part of CIT in 2008. By 2012, the Silicon Valley campus enrollment exceeded 150 in master's programs in software engineering, software management, engineering and technology innovation management, and information technology, as well as a bicoastal Ph.D. program in electrical and computer engineering with a focus on mobility offered in conjunction with the new CyLab Mobility Research Center.

> **Diversity**
> The number of women and minority graduate students in CIT between 2004 and 2011 grew from 218 to 387.

James H. Garrett, Jr. Photo by Mireille Mobley.

Educating the Engineers of the Future

The Carnegie Plan emphasized the role of educational institutions not just in training engineers but in helping students who become engineers to continue learning throughout life, becoming leaders in their communities.

In keeping with those tenets, in 2011, CIT began "innovation across the curriculum," a reassessment of the general educational elements of undergraduate engineering education. With the full support of all colleges within CMU, a committee comprised of

James H. Garrett, Jr.
Dean of Engineering, 2013-
Jim Garrett, the Thomas Lord Professor of Civil and Environmental Engineering at CMU, received his B.S. in 1982, his M.S. in 1983 and his Ph.D. in 1986, all in civil engineering from CMU. He worked for Schlumberger Well Services in the Houston Downhole Sensors Division from 1986 to 1987 and was an assistant professor at the University of Illinois at Urbana-Champaign from 1987 to 1990. After joining CMU in 1990, he served as associate dean for Academic Affairs from 2000 to 2006 and as head of the Department of Civil and Environmental Engineering from 2006 to 2012. He became dean of CIT in 2013.
From 2005 to 2010, Garrett was faculty co-director of the Center for Sensed Critical Infrastructure (CenSCIR). CenSCIR became the PSII—Pennsylvania Smart Infrastructure Incubator in 2010, with support from IBM, Bombardier and the Commonwealth of Pennsylvania. Garrett was PSII faculty co-director until becoming dean in 2013. Garrett is a fellow of the American Society of Civil Engineers (ASCE).
The author of more than 250 publications, Garrett was awarded the 2007 Steven J. Fenves Award for Systems Research at Carnegie Mellon, the 2006 ASCE Computing in Civil Engineering Award, and the ASCE Journal of Computing in Civil Engineering Best Paper Award in 2001.

Announcement of Sherman and Joyce Bowie Scott Hall, to be completed in 2015. Photo by Leah Pileggi.

representatives of every engineering discipline established guidelines to help broaden CIT's engineering undergraduate curriculum preparing students to take their technical knowledge out into the global community to establish companies and contribute to society on a larger scale. In essence, CIT's enhanced curriculum will help students to think big by supplying both the scientific/technical and humanistic/social background to support their dreams.

A Change of Scenery

Perhaps in the future, the physical space of universities will be less important than the amount and quality of electronic distance learning it offers. Nonetheless, a new CIT building on campus—the Sherman and Joyce Bowie Scott Hall—will provide much needed space, housing the Wilton E. Scott Institute for Energy Innovation, the Biomedical Engineering Department and a state-of-the-art nanofabrication facility. An estimated two hundred faculty members and students are scheduled to be based in the building that is anticipated to be completed in 2014.

The design of the new building, while modern, is charged with embodying the spirit that Henry Hornbostel intended for the original Carnegie Technical Schools.

Could anyone in 1900 have realistically anticipated today's research that borders on science fiction or the range of programs offered under the umbrella of engineering or the numbers and diversity of engineering students now enrolled in CIT? Not even Andrew Carnegie. In fact, he would be surprised that the driving force behind the founding of the Carnegie Technical Schools—steel—no longer rules the Pittsburgh region. Now it's high tech and education and medicine, and a lot of growth in those areas can be attributed to the rich and deep history of CIT preparing graduates to use their knowledge for problem solving, collaboration and responsible citizenship.

Andrew Carnegie would be proud.

MECHANICAL ENGINEERING. Students in Professor Shelley Anna's research lab work on experimental fluid dynamics. Photo by Tim Kaulen.

BIOMEDICAL ENGINEERING. The BME logo was designed in 2008 by department head Yu-li Wang. Hidden within the structure of a DNA-like double helix are the letters B, M, and E.

MATERIALS SCIENCE AND ENGINEERING. The undergraduate educational program in Materials Science and Engineering emphasizes the laboratory experience. This room, which served as the machine shop for six decades, has been redeployed as an undergraduate laboratory.

CIVIL AND ENVIRONMENTAL ENGINEERING. Students Dan Little, Raymond Naula, Andrew Klein, Sarah Ramp and Jule Carr utilize the teaching flume to examine characteristics of open-channel flow in Professor Kelvin Gregory's fluid mechanics laboratory course. Photo by Mireille Mobley.

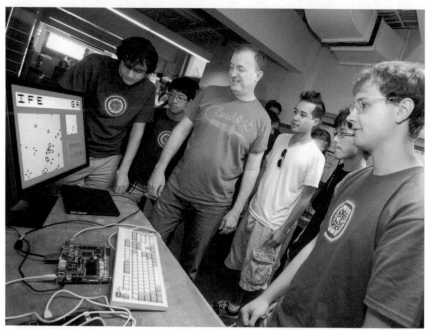

ELECTRICAL AND COMPUTER ENGINEERING. ECE students and faculty take part in the annual student-led "Build 18" project design and demonstration fair, a week in which students build, tinker and speed-hack projects that solve real problems. Photo by Larry Rippel.

CHEMICAL ENGINEERING. An open, shared lab in chemical engineering. Photo by Ken Andreyo.

SILICON VALLEY. Carnegie Mellon Silicon Valley celebrates its 10th anniversary in 2012, graduating its 650th student at its diploma ceremony in August. Photo by Amy Harrity.

ENGINEERING AND PUBLIC POLICY. Jay Apt introduces Chris Trueblood, of the Electric Power Research Institute, at the Carnegie Mellon Electricity Industry Center biweekly seminar series on November 14, 2012.

INFORMATION NETWORKING INSTITUTE. The Information Networking Institute's 20th Anniversary, April 17, 2010. Celebrating two decades of academic excellence and innovation. Photo by Larry Rippel.

CARNEGIE MELLON UNIVERSITY IN RWANDA. Carnegie Mellon University in Rwanda is the first U.S. research institution offering degrees in Africa with an in-country presence. Photograph by Crystal Rugege.

References

Anderson, John Miller. *Workshop of Engineers*. New York: General Electric Company, 1953.

Boucher, John N. *A Century and a Half of Pittsburg and Her People*. Vol. 2. New York: Lewis Publishing Company, 1908. Full text available from the University of Pittsburgh, Digital Research Library, Historic Pittsburgh, http://digital.library.pitt.edu/cgi-bin/t/text/text-idx?idno=02awn7797m;view=toc;c=pitttext.

Carnegie, Andrew. *Autobiography of Andrew Carnegie*. London: Constable and Co., Ltd., 1920.

Carnegie Institute of Technology. *Education for Professional Responsibility*. Pittsburgh: Carnegie Press, 1948.

Carnegie Mellon University. *Carnegie Mellon University Factbook, 2012–2013, Volume 27*. Pittsburgh: Carnegie Mellon University, 2013.

Cleeton, G. E. *The Doherty Administration, 1936–1950*. Pittsburgh: Carnegie Press, Carnegie Institute of Technology, 1965.

Department of Electrical and Computer Engineering. *A New Undergraduate Curriculum*. Pittsburgh: Carnegie Mellon University, 1991.

Department of Engineering and Public Policy. *Annual Reports of the Program in Engineering and Public Affairs* (later the Program in Engineering and Public Policy and now the Department of Engineering and Public Policy). Pittsburgh: CIT, Carnegie Mellon University.

Director, Stephen W., Pradeep K. Khosla, Ronald A. Rohrer, and Rob A. Rutenbar. "Reengineering the Curriculum: Design and Analysis of a new Undergraduate Electrical and Computer Engineering Degree at Carnegie Mellon University." *Proceedings of the IEEE* 83, no. 9 (September 1995): 1246–69.

Edge, Laura B. *Andrew Carnegie: Industrial Philanthropist*. Minneapolis: Lerner Publications Company, 2004.

Fenton, Edwin. *Carnegie Mellon 1900–2000: A Centennial History*. Pittsburgh: Carnegie Mellon University Press, 2000.

Hacker, Louis M. *The World of Andrew Carnegie, 1865–1901*. Philadelphia: J. B. Lippincott Company, 1968.

Hamerschlag, Arthur A. "The Education of Electrical Apprentices and Journeymen." Presented at the 130th Meeting of American Institute of Electrical Engineers, New York, 28 December 1898.

In Memory of Andrew Carnegie: His Life and Work, 1835–1919. Full text available from the Carnegie Collection, http://diva.library.cmu.edu/webapp/carnegie/item.jsp?q=acc/box00002/fld00029/bdl0001/doc0001.

Joselit, Jenna Weissman. "Notice! Getting Under the Cheerful Surface of Historical Signage." *Tablet Magazine,* 13 January 2009.

Nobel Media. "The Sveriges Riksbank Prize in Economic Sciences in Memory of Alfred Nobel 1978: Herbert A. Simon." Nobelrprize.org. http://www.nobelprize.org/nobel_prizes/economic-sciences/laureates/1978/simon.html.

Reynolds, Terry S., ed. *The Engineer in America: A Historical Anthology from Technology and Culture.* Chicago: University of Chicago Press, 1991.

Rothfus, Robert R. *The History of Chemical Engineering at Carnegie Mellon University.* Pittsburgh: Carnegie Mellon University, 1982.

Schaefer, Ludwig F. *Evolution of a National Research University: The Stever Administration and the Cyert Years at Carnegie Mellon, 1965–1990.* Pittsburgh: Carnegie Mellon University Press, 1992.

Sell, George. "Oral-History: Benjamin Richard Teare, Jr." IEEE History Center, New Brunswick, NJ, 28 December 1979. http://www.ieeeghn.org/wiki/index.php/Oral-History:Benjamin_R._Teare_Jr.

Semiconductor Research Corporation. "SRC Milestones: 1982." http://www.src.org/src/story/timeline/1982/.

Servos, John W. "Changing Partners: The Mellon Institute, Private Industry and the Federal Patron." *Technology and Culture* 34 (1994): 221–57.

Simon, Herbert A. *The Sciences of the Artificial.* Cambridge: MIT Press, 1996.

Tappan, E. M. *Andrew Carnegie's Own Story.* Comprised of a series of condensed chapters from *The Autobiography of Andrew Carnegie.* Edinburgh, Scotland: Holmes McDouglall Limited, 1920.

Tarbell, A. W. *The Story of Carnegie Tech, Being a History of Carnegie Institute of Technology from 1900 to 1935.* Pittsburgh: Carnegie Institute Press, 1937.

Ver Planck, D. W. *Engineering Analysis.* New York: John Wiley and Sons, 1952.

Westerberg, Arthur W., and Carnegie Mellon University Engineering Design Research Center. "Applications of AI in Design Research at Carnegie Mellon University's EDRC." Department of Chemical Engineering, Paper 141, 1989.

Wright, Austin. *The Warner Administration at Carnegie Institute of Technology, 1950–1965.* Pittsburgh: Carnegie Press, 1973.

Interviews

Anderson, John L. Telephone Interview. 22 Oct. 2010.

Director, Stephen W. Telephone Interview. 18 Oct. 2010.

Fenves, Steven J. Telephone Interview. 8 Sept. 2010.

Grossmann, Ignacio. Personal Interview. 9 May 2013.

Jordan, Angel G. Personal Interview. 24 Aug. 2010.

Mathias, Bob. Telephone Interview. 1 Sept. 2011.

McMichael, Francis C. Personal Interview. 1 Dec. 2010.

Moura, José M. F. Personal Interview. 10 May 2013.

Paxton, Harold W. Telephone Interview. 21 Jan. 2011.

Rouleau, Wilfred T. Personal Interview. 10 Nov. 2010.

Tarr, Joel A. Personal Interview. 2 Dec. 2010.

Westerberg, Arthur W. Telephone Interview. 17 Nov. 2010.

Williams, James C. Telephone Interview. 19 Oct. 2010.